SOCIAL STUDIES LEVEL 3

Exploring People and the Past

Ed Offer

Series Editor: Ollie Bray

HODDER
GIBSON

The Publishers would like to thank the following for permission to reproduce copyright material:

Photo credits p.4 © Hodder Gibson; p.5 © National Library of Scotland/Scran; p.6 © Photofusion Picture Library/Alamy; p.9 © LABAT Jean Michel/Sunset/Rex Features; p.10 (both) © National Museums Scotland/Scran; p.11 © Orkney Islands Council/Scran; p.12 (t) © Patrick Dieudonne/Robert Harding World Imagery/Corbis, (b) © Ros Drinkwater/Alamy; p.16 © The Art Archive/Alamy; p.17 Courtesy of Wikipedia; p.18 © Hodder Gibson; p.19 (t) © Nikreates/Alamy, (b) © The Granger Collection, New York/Topfoto; p.23 © Yoshio Tomii Photo Studio/Photolibrary; p.25 © Ivy Close Images/Alamy; p.27 © Bobbi Tull/Photolibrary; p.31 © INTERFOTO/Alamy; p.34 © Girolamo Macchietti/Getty Images; p.36 (main) © Travelshots.com/Alamy, (inset) © The Vindolanda Trust; p.37 © National Library of Scotland/Scran; p.39 (t) © David Robertson/Alamy, (c) © Norman Price/Alamy, (b) © David Kilpatrick/Alamy; p.41 © Robert Harding World Imagery/Corbis; p.43 © Look and Learn/Bridgeman Art Library; p.44 © Hodder Gibson; p.45 © Mary Evans Picture Library/Alamy; p.46 © INTERFOTO/Alamy; p.47 © INTERFOTO/Alamy; p.49 © Cruck Cottage Heritage Association/www.cruckcottage. com; p.50 © Ed Offer; p.52 (l) © IMAGEPAST/Alamy, (r) © Rex Features; p.53 © Paul Fawcett/ iStockphoto.com; p.54 © Hodder Gibson; p.56 © David Robertson/Alamy; p.57 (t) © DAVID MOIR/Reuters/Corbis, (b) © Robert Harding Picture Library Ltd/Alamy; p.59 © Topfoto; p.60 (t) © Heiner Heine/Photolibrary, (c, l to r) © Brownstock Inc./Alamy, © JP Laffont/Sygma/CORBIS, © Blend Images/Alamy, © Mai Chen/Alamy, (b) © Art Directors & TRIP/Alamy; p.63 © Topfoto; p.64 © The Art Archive/Alamy; p.67 © The British Library/Photolibrary; p.68 © doughoughton/Alamy; p.70 © Topfoto; p.71 © 2d Alan King/Alamy; p.72 © Alan King engraving/Alamy; p.74 (t) © Pictorial Press Ltd/Alamy, (b) © John Hume/ Scran; p.75 © Pictorial Press Ltd/Alamy; p.76 © M.Brodie/Alamy; p.77 (l) © M.Brodie/Alamy, (r) © Classic Image/Alamy; p.78 © North Wind Picture Archives/Alamy; p.79 (t) © Lebrecht Music and Arts Photo Library/Alamy, (b) © INTERFOTO/ Alamy; p.81 (tl) © Ivy Close Images/Alamy, (bl) © The Gallery Collection/Corbis, (r) © Hulton-Deutsch Collection/ CORBIS; p.84 © Oscar Gutierrez/Alamy; p.85 © Topfoto; p.86 © Blend Images/Alamy; p.87 (t) © Topfoto, (b) © NASA – digital version copyright/Science Faction/Corbis; p.88 Annie Reynolds/Photodisc/Getty Images; p.89 (t) © North Wind Picture Archives/Alamy, (b) © 19th era/Alamy; p.90 (t) © Classic Image/Alamy, (b) © Hodder Gibson; p.91 © Bettmann/ CORBIS; p.97 © The National Trust Photolibrary/Alamy; p.98 © Stapleton Historical Collection/Photolibrary; p.99 (t) © Mary Evans Picture Library/Alamy, (b) © Mary Evans Picture Library; p.100 © Hodder Gibson; p.104 © Kim Kulish/ Corbis; p.105 (l) © Proehl Studios/Corbis, (r) © STUART WALKER/Alamy; p.106 © Design Pics Inc./Alamy; p.108 (both) © Google 2010; p.109 (both) © Google 2010; p.110 (t) © Chen Gang/Xinhua Press/Corbis, (b) © James Brittain/VIEW/ Corbis; p.111 © Graham Beckram; p.113 (both) © Graham Beckram; p.114 © Louise Gubb/Corbis; p.115 US Geological Survey Image NASA, © Google; p.116 (l) © STEVE LINDRIDGE/Alamy, (r) image © 2010TerraMetrics, © 2010 Google; p.117 (both) Image © 2010 GeoEye, © 2009 Google; p.118 © Jen Deyenberg; p.119 (l) © Jen Deyenberg, (r) © 2010 Tele Atlas © 2009 Google.

Every effort has been made to trace all copyright holders, but if any have been inadvertently overlooked the Publishers will be pleased to make the necessary arrangements at the first opportunity.

Although every effort has been made to ensure that website addresses are correct at time of going to press, Hodder Gibson cannot be held responsible for the content of any website mentioned in this book. It is sometimes possible to find a relocated web page by typing in the address of the home page for a website in the URL window of your browser.

Hachette Livre UK's policy is to use papers that are natural, renewable and recyclable products and made from wood grown in sustainable forests. The logging and manufacturing processes are expected to conform to the environmental regulations of the country of origin.

Orders: please contact Bookpoint Ltd, 130 Milton Park, Abingdon, Oxon OX14 4SB. Telephone: (44) 01235 827720. Fax: (44) 01235 400454. Lines are open 9.00–5.00, Monday to Saturday, with a 24-hour message answering service. Visit our website at www.hoddereducation.co.uk. Hodder Gibson can be contacted direct on: Tel: 0141 848 1609; Fax: 0141 889 6315; email: hoddergibson@hodder.co.uk

© Ed Offer 2010
First published in 2010 by
Hodder Gibson, an imprint of Hodder Education,
An Hachette UK Company
2a Christie Street
Paisley PA1 1NB

Impression number	5 4 3 2 1
Year	2014 2013 2012 2011 2010

Cover photo © Kuttig–Travel–2/Alamy
Illustrations by Metaphrog, Jeff Edwards and Emma Golley (Redmoor Design)
Typeset in 11pt Stone Serif by DC Graphic Design Limited
Printed in Italy

A catalogue record for this title is available from the British Library

ISBN: 978 1444 112788

Contents

1 Why should I learn about people, past events and societies?

What are we exploring?

By the end of this section you should be able to:

▶ Explain at least one reason why we should study the past
▶ Argue why the past is important
▶ Imagine what the world would be like if we knew nothing about the past

History is just dates, battles and dead folk.

Look at the statement on the left. Of course, those things are in this book, but there is so much more to explore. History is really the study of the most fascinating topic on the planet – people. For two million years advanced apes called 'humans' have ruled the Earth. The story of these humans is a cracking read but is also really important for *your* future!

How can dead people help me with my future?

History is the memories of people in the past and we still have plenty to learn from their experiences. This book will help you find out about your own origins and those of your friends, family, fellow Scots and peoples of the world! Not much to explore then!

Activate your brain cells!

What does learning from experience mean?

- Imagine all the people in your class wrote down their own experiences of a particular event in a web blog. For example, if everyone wrote about their first day at secondary school.
- Why might those blogs be useful to look at as evidence of what day one was like?
- Would there be any problems with using the blogs as evidence?

Show your understanding

1. Think about these students' statements. Which one do you like the most?
2. Write a list of the statements and rank them, with the one you like most at the top and the one you are not interested in at the bottom.
3. Share your ideas with the rest of the class and your teacher. Can you reach an agreement on one statement that best explains the importance of History?

What other reasons are there for studying the past?

Read what previous students have said about History:

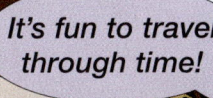

It's fun to travel through time!

All the social subjects teach you the skills to get a good job.

History joins up with Geography and Modern Studies to help me discover how my community, country and world have developed.

History helps me learn the skills to think for myself and not believe everything I read or hear.

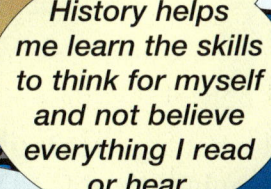

How can I know my future if I don't know my past?

History makes you realise that people in the past were not just 'good' or 'bad', but did things for different reasons, just like us.

History lets you discover how and why people behaved as they did, whether they are John Lennon or Hitler.

Finding out about the development of culture, music, art, books, science, mathematics, food, clothes and technology helps me to make connections with my life now.

Collect a skill

origin
evidence past
experience
history

Collect a skill

Here we will focus on the skills you will learn in History, which you will get better at as we go through the book. Keep your skills work somewhere safe – the back of your jotter is a good idea. These are not simply subject skills but skills you will need throughout school and in life. Who says History is not important?

Increase your word power

You will come across many words in this book that you may not have read or heard before. Learning how to spell them and what they mean will increase your word power and really help you communicate.

1. When you find a word in **bold** or an historical idea you don't understand, record it in a list. Explain its meaning in words and/or pictures. Ask your teacher or use dictionaries or encyclopedias to help you understand the meaning. Here is one way of doing this:

Keyword	Definition – what does it mean?	Illustration

2. Do this for all the chapters in the book to **boost your skill level!**

2 You're history!

By the end of this section you should be able to:

▶ Understand how you are directly linked to the past
▶ Describe ways you can find out about the history of your community

Activate your brain cells!

- List all the words and pictures that you can think of to do with the word 'community'.
- Create a class spider diagram or Post-it note diagram with 'community' written in the middle.
- Add the word 'community' to your vocabulary list and find a definition in a dictionary.

> You are part of what people in the future will call 'history'. You are connected to the past and to the future. You are history!

The past is all around you. It is in the buildings you see in your **community**, the songs you listen to, the clothes you wear and the tools and technology you use. All the things you think are good and bad have developed from the ideas and experiences of people who came before you.

Everything you do today will add to these ideas and experiences.

How can I find out about the history of my family?

Your family were a fascinating bunch! What do you know about them?

- The older people in your family will have stories about your **relatives**. How could you record these stories?
- Did any relatives fight in the wars of the last century?
- Have you got any famous relatives?
- Do you have any old pictures or documents at home you could bring in and show?

- Find out what a **genealogist** does and how they might be able to help you.

How can I find out about the history of my community?

We can find out about our community's past in a number of ways. Here are some ideas:

SOURCE A

Source A is a picture of a tenement building in Glasgow. We want to know when it was built and who has lived there. How can we find out answers to these questions?

Now look at Sources B and C. For each source, try to work out what it is and explain how it can help us find some answers to our questions about the tenement.

SOURCE B

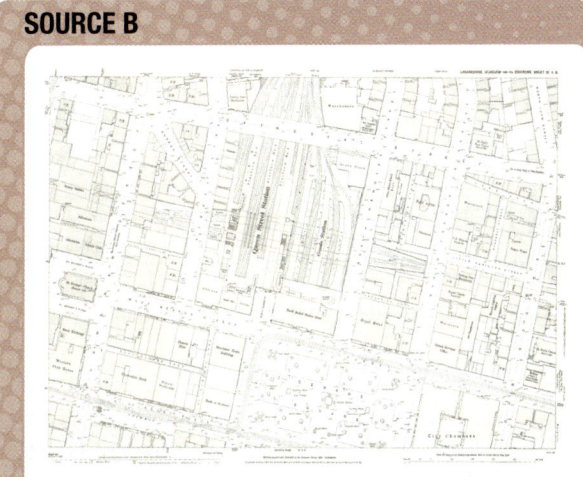

Sources of information about your local area	Rank	What can it/they tell us?
Local library		
People		
Archaeologists		
Textbooks		
Paintings		
Photographs		
Film		
Local radio station		
Maps		
Accounts		
Church records (births, marriages and deaths)		
Legal records		
Government census		
Buildings		
Diaries		
Letters		
Bills		
Place names		
Ruins and remains		
TV programmes		
Local museums		
Graveyards		

🧩 Show your understanding

1. Copy the table opposite into your jotter and complete it by ranking the twenty sources of information in order of usefulness for finding out about the tenement. Put the most useful source as number one.
2. Complete the last column – what can the sources tell us?

SOURCE C

Name of street/ road, and name or no. of house or flat	Name and surname of each person who lived in the house, on the night of 30 May 1871	Relation to head of family	Age	Profession or occupation	Where born
15A MacDonald Road	Frank O'Connor	Head	42	Riveter, Clyde Dockyard	Belfast, Ireland
	Monica O'Connor	Wife	27		Glasgow
	William O'Connor	Son	10		Glasgow
	Liam O'Connor	Son	8		Glasgow
	Erin O'Connor	Daughter	6		Glasgow
	Roisin O'Connor	Daughter	5		Glasgow
	Colm O'Connor	Son	3		Glasgow

3 Get out and about

What are we exploring?

By the end of this section you should be able to:

▶ Produce a film about your community

▶ Use cameras and video-editing applications

▶ Describe how you might improve your finished movie

In groups, your mission is to make a ten-minute film or podcast about the community you live in.

Planning

Ten minutes is not a long time, so good planning is essential.

- What do you know already about your home city, town or village?
- What stories about your community's past should be told?
- Where could you go for more information?
- Who could you ask for more information?
- If you live in a town or village with a main high street, create a treasure hunt walk that points out interesting facts about the buildings and your community.

Think about where you want to film each scene and what you want to film there. Here is an example plan:

Scene 1: *High street*	**Scene 2:** *What the buildings tell us*	**Scene 3:** *Our hidden town*
Scene 4: *What the graveyard can tell us*	**Scene 5:** *Our landscape*	**Scene 6:** *Famous people from our community*

Filming tips

1. Be creative and have fun!
2. If you have old photographs, take pictures of the scene as it looks now and edit the two together to show how your community has changed.
3. Interview people about the community and its past.
4. Remember – good presentations are about quality not quantity. Make sure what you are filming is well lit and hold the camera steady if you don't have a tripod.
5. If it is windy or noisy outside, your camera may not pick up what people are saying. Move them closer to the camera or film elsewhere to improve the sound quality.
6. Keep any comedy moments for an out-takes section during the credits!

REVIEW

- How did your film turn out?
- What are you proud of?
- What would you change next time?

- What new skills have you learnt?
- How could you use these skills in the future?

Treasure hunt competition

- Make a copy of this treasure hunt grid.
- Go out in your local community and find the objects on the sheet.
- Stick objects onto your grid using sellotape.
- Keep interviews in a folder or save them electronically.

Editing and publishing

- You can edit the footage on Macs using Imovie™ or on PCs using MovieMaker™.
- Add a title and credits.
- Put your own music over the video.
- Publish the video on your school website.

	Names of your great-grandparents	Date your school was built	Oldest coin you can find
Plan of your house and garden			
An old picture of your high street	Oldest building in your high street	The words on the oldest gravestone you can find	
Picture of an object in nearest museum	Name of hospital where you were born	Picture of your family	
Name of your nearest church	Interview with an older person about their school life	Photo of you as a baby	
A leaflet from nearest museum	A new picture of your high street	A story from your community's past	

4 Why did people move here?

By the end of this section you should be able to:

▶ Explain at least one reason why people moved to Scotland

▶ Imagine and describe what the first people were like

 Activate your brain cells!

Humans are really young! If the entire length of our planet's life were seen as a single day, human beings would probably only appear in the last second before midnight! However, the land we walk upon is **ancient** and has been changed by the weather over millions of years.

Study this diagram. It is called a **timeline**. What does it show?

15,000 years ago the land we now call Scotland was covered in a sheet of ice hundreds of metres thick. As it moved, it shaped the land underneath. Mountains, rivers, glens, lochs and bogs were formed.

Gradually, plants began to grow and spread. The first forests of birch, hazel and rowan trees appeared in 8000BC. Eventually insects, birds and animals arrived and the low ground became green grassland.

The first people appeared from around 7000BC. They moved across the land, through the dark forests and along the coasts to find food and somewhere safe to settle for a while. There were not many, only five or six hundred of them. This was the **Mesolithic** or **Middle Stone Age**.

The Big Bang?
4.5 billion years ago

First evidence of oceans and life
3.5 billion years ago

The first cells with a nucleus
1.7 billion years ago

The age of dinosaurs
0.3 billion years ago

Earth's core forms
4.2 billion years ago

The oldest rock forms
4 billion years ago

Rise in Earth's oxygen levels
2.5 billion years ago

The first hard-shelled animals
0.5 billion years ago

The first humans
(Stone Age man)

What do we know about the first people to settle in Scotland?

Archaeologists have helped us find out more about these Mesolithic people. During **excavations** of ancient sites they have found tools made from animal bones, rocks and antlers. These showed that they were hunters.

Other objects have been found in their **middens** – hooks, pins, harpoon heads and shaped stones. Remains of nuts, berries, plants and shellfish tell us what they gathered to eat. Rare cave paintings also help us understand more. Apart from these finds, there is very little evidence of these people. Their clothes and blankets, ropes and baskets were made mostly of animal skins and have rotted away.

At 16,000 years old, the cave paintings found at Lasceaux in France are thought to be the oldest known paintings in the world.

The cavemen myth

What do you think cavemen looked like?

Most people think of the first man as rough, tough and brutal. He uses few words and drags a woman along by her hair, waiting as she cooks his food and brings up his children.

The truth about cavemen

In History the truth is always much more interesting. The men did do most of the dangerous hunting, but families could not live on dead animals alone because their flesh quickly became rotten. Women had the equally important job of collecting berries, nuts and herbs to feed the family.

Women also had the most important **responsibility** of bringing up children. Women and men probably worked as partners, relying on each others' skills.

4 Why did people move here? (cont.)

 Show your understanding

1 How many years did it take for the first humans to appear on Earth?
2 Why did the first people move into the land we now call Scotland? What were they looking for?
3 Look at Sources A and B. What can they tell us about the people who used them?
4 Complete either a) or b).
   a) Copy all of the following sentences. Then, next to each sentence write if it is true or false. If you believe the sentence is false, write a correct sentence underneath.
      • Human beings have lived on Earth for only a short length of time.
      • The landscape of Scotland was formed by moving ice.
      • Mesolithic people only ate berries and plants.
      • Archaeologists have found clothes that the cavemen wore.
      • Mesolithic men were the head of the family and dominated women.
   b) Design your own version of a Mesolithic cave painting like the one on page 9.

Source A Why was this object made?

Source B What might these have been used for?

Collect a skill – understanding sources

You have looked at some sources here. Historians use sources to help them piece together the truth about the past. The next skill to learn is the difference between **primary** and **secondary** sources.

Primary source – this means that the source was written, created or spoken around the time of the event you are studying. A diary is an example of a primary source.

Secondary source – this means that the source was written, created or spoken well after the event you are studying. This textbook is an example of a secondary source.

Top Tip – primary sources are not always better than secondary sources. The sources have to be investigated for the truth, no matter when they were created. You will learn this skill later!

1. Copy the definition of a primary and secondary source for your own notes. You will need to come back to this many times in your studies!

2. Write down any examples of primary and secondary sources you can find on this page.

3. Flick through the textbook – find examples of both types of sources. Ask your teacher for help if you are having trouble.

? Bore your friends...

The first modern humans appeared 135,000 years ago in Africa. They have since been named Homo sapiens, which means 'wise men' in Latin. They were much more advanced than the European Neanderthals, who eventually died out 40,000 years ago!

5 What secrets were uncovered at Skara Brae?

What are we exploring?

By the end of this section you should be able to:
▶ Explain what was found at Skara Brae
▶ Describe how different this community was to your own
▶ Imagine what happened to this community

⚙ Activate your brain cells!

- Imagine you suddenly have to leave home and time-travel to the year AD2400. You only have enough room to take ten essential items from this list. What will you need?

Calculator	Radio	French dictionary	Heavy shoes
Tape recorder	Television	Chinese phrasebook	Raincoat
Warm clothes	DVD player	Camera	Watch
Cash	Games console	Notebook	Sleeping bag
Sunglasses	English dictionary	Bicycle	Food

- Compare your lists with someone else – are your lists different? If so, why?
- If you could only take two items, which ones would you take?

From cavemen to farmers!

Historians think that the next big change for humans happened around 4000BC. This was when more people moved to Scotland from all over Europe. These people knew how to farm as well as how to hunt. They brought animals with them in their boats, such as pigs, cows and sheep. They also brought and grew wheat and barley grain. They built large **settlements** like Skara Brae. This period of time has been called the **Neolithic** or **New Stone Age**.

What happened at Skara Brae?

In 1850, a violent gale ripped across the islands of Orkney off the north coast of Scotland. The sand on part of the Orkney Mainland coast was blown away. This revealed an amazing Neolithic settlement that had been buried under the sand for nearly 5000 years. The people who found the settlement named it Skara Brae.

A room in Skara Brae

Archaeologists think around 50 people once lived there. The eight underground houses give us evidence about the lives of Neolithic people. The houses are connected by covered passageways. Everything was made of stone. The people had box beds made from stone slabs, shelves, cupboards for food, personal belongings and even a simple toilet.

Middens show the people were skilled farmers who grew their own food and made their own tools and pottery. The discarded bones of cattle, sheep and pigs are evidence that the community reared its own animals.

There are no human remains at Skara Brae. Evidence shows that the community left quickly and never returned. A last meal was left cooking in a pot, valuable tools and dyes were abandoned, a precious bead necklace lay scattered on the floor. We may never know what terror made the people flee so quickly. What do you think happened?

Collect a skill

Recognising change and continuity

History shows us how the world has changed. Yet some things also stay the same. Understanding the importance of **change** and **continuity** in the past is a key skill to understanding where you are in time.

Bring old photographs of you to show your classmates. How have you changed since the photo was taken? What new ideas and possessions do you have? Has anything or anyone in your life stayed the same from that time?

1. Find old photographs of your community. Search online for old pictures of your street, school, high street or local buildings – black and white photographs would be best for this.

2. Try to work out what has **changed**. Why has it changed?

   a) What has **stayed the same** and why?

   b) Think about how you live now – will it be the same in a few years? How will things have changed? How will you have changed? Will anything have continued to stay the same?

 Show your understanding

1 Draw a table like the one below and complete it using the information about Skara Brae.

Evidence from Skara Brae	What does it tell us about the people of Skara Brae?	Is this different from how we live today?	Is this similar to how we live today?
Eight underground houses connected together	More than one family lived in this settlement. There was a community.	Yes, because...	No

2 How different was life in Skara Brae from your life today?

3 Choose either task a) or b).

   a) Imagine you are living in Skara Brae 5000 years ago. Write three entries in your diary to describe how you live, why you had to leave and how you feel about the experience.

   b) Create a storyboard of the events at Skara Brae. Show how people lived and some of the objects they had 5000 years ago. Show the people fleeing the settlement and include pictures showing your own idea about why they fled.

6 How did metal change everything?

What are we exploring?

By the end of this section you should be able to:

▶ Explain why the discovery of metal was so important for humans

▶ Describe how different metals were used

▶ Imagine how different life would be without this discovery

Activate your brain cells!

Look around your classroom. How many things made out of metal can you see?

- Now list five metal objects used at home. How essential are these objects to you?
- How important is metal to us? Discuss this with the rest of your class.

The discovery of metal

One of humankind's most important discoveries was when Stone Age people worked out how to get metal from rocks. Metal **ore** was melted and poured into moulds. It was then cooled to make a solid shape and taken out of the mould.

People quickly developed clever ways of making tools, jewellery, pottery and weapons with three different types of metal – copper, tin and iron. It changed their way of life forever.

Archaeologists have divided the time before written history into three ages based on when these metals were discovered by humans. These are the **Stone Age**, followed by the **Bronze Age** and finally the **Iron Age**.

Show your understanding

1. Choose to answer either a) or b).
   a) Explain in your own words how bronze is made.
      Use Source A to help you.
   b) Draw a diagram to explain how bronze is made.
2. How did the discovery of metal change the lives of Stone Age people?
3. Below are the names of the first seven metals discovered, but their letters have been jumbled up. Unscramble them and try to place them in order of value, with the most valuable first.
   **PCOPRE   ITN   EDAL   DOGL
   RONI   YURMERC   VILERS**

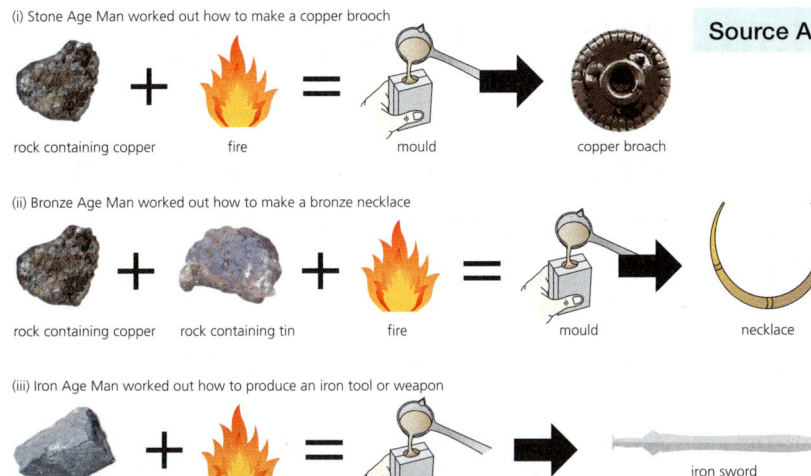

(i) Stone Age Man worked out how to make a copper brooch

rock containing copper + fire = mould → copper broach

(ii) Bronze Age Man worked out how to make a bronze necklace

rock containing copper + rock containing tin + fire = mould → necklace

(iii) Iron Age Man worked out how to produce an iron tool or weapon

rock containing iron ore + fire = mould → iron sword

Source A

Metal rocks!

Today there are 86 metals known to scientists. Many of them have weird and wonderful names – quiz your **science teacher** to see if they know them all!

Most metals were not discovered until the last century, so for 7000 years only seven metals were known to man. These metals were important to the growth and wealth of many ancient civilisations from the **Mesopotamians** to the **Egyptians**, **Greeks** and **Romans**.

Collect a skill

Understanding chronology

Understanding what happened in the past can be confusing. Historians have to talk of times being '**approximate**' because we sometimes do not know exactly when things happened. Events don't happen in a straight line.

For example, there are tribes living today in New Guinea and Brazil that are at the same stage of development as the men of Stone Age Europe were. They use simple weapons to hunt and stone tools to prepare food. Yet they live in a world where men have the technology to go into space!

In the same way, European Stone Age men living in a remote part of Scotland were still using stone axes long after their neighbours were making metal tools. Not everything changes at once when something new is discovered.

To understand a story you must know what order things happened in. This is called putting things in **chronological order** – the order in which things happened.

Show your understanding

1. What does **chronological order** mean?
2. Put the following events in the order in which they happened.
   - The discovery of metal
   - Scotland covered by ice
   - Skara Brae occupied by Stone Age people
   - Neolithic farmers arrive in Scotland
   - Mesolithic hunters settle in Scotland
   - Remains of Skara Brae discovered
3. Modern European historians have divided the past into the periods set out below. Can you arrange them in the correct chronological order?
   - Early Modern Times (AD1500 to AD1700)
   - Modern Times (AD1700 to today)
   - Bronze Age (2400BC to 700BC)
   - Neolithic Stone Age (4300BC to 2400BC)
   - Middle Ages (AD409 to AD1500)
   - Iron Age (700BC to AD45)
   - Roman Britain (AD45 to AD409)

7 What is a civilisation?

What are we exploring?

By the end of this section you should be able to:
▶ Explain what a civilisation is
▶ Describe what ancient Mesopotamia was like
▶ Imagine what it was like to live in ancient Mesopotamia

A society that is not backward or basic is called a **civilisation**. Civilised people think that respect, knowledge and good government are important.

The first real civilisation appeared around 3500BC, between the rivers Euphrates and Tigris in modern-day Iraq. The people living here were some of the first to learn to farm and use metals, and their knowledge spread as they traded with other peoples. The group of towns and cities became known as the **Mesopotamian Civilisation**, which means 'between the rivers'.

Activate your brain cells!

- Have you ever heard someone call another person civilised? What does it mean?
- Why might different people have different ideas about what is civilised? Discuss with a partner and feed back to the class.

Fascinating facts about the Mesopotamians

It hardly ever rained in Mesopotamia but, when it did, the two rivers burst their banks. So the Mesopotamian people invented **canals** and **dams** to get water from the rivers to their fields and prevent flooding.

Canals provided more water for the crops – this meant more could be grown. More crops led to more food for the people. More food meant families could think about becoming bigger by having more children, so the population increased.

There was so much food that not everyone had to farm. Kings, priests, teachers, traders, guards, soldiers and other jobs appeared.

Writing developed in Mesopotamia before anywhere else. They wrote their words and numbers on flat blocks of wet clay called **tablet**, using the tip of a reed or a wooden stick. The tip was carved into a wedge shape, like a little arrow, and pressed into the tablet to make a mark.

The ancient word for wedge-shaped was **cuneiform** and this style of writing is known as cuneiform writing.

— Present-day bound

Mesopotamians built massive temples called **Ziggurats**, which could be up to 30 metres tall. King **Nebuchadnezzar** of the Mesopotamian city of Babylon built a huge Ziggurat tower with a temple on top. The tower's sides held the Hanging Gardens – one of the seven wonders of the ancient world.

The **decimal point** was used by Mesopotamian mathematicians. They were the first to divide an hour into 60 minutes and a minute into 60 seconds.

Pottery has been found all over Europe and the Far East that was made in Mesopotamia. Pots were mass-produced using **potter's wheels**. By 3000BC the Mesopotamians had worked out how to use the wheel to transport items around.

King **Hammurabi** of Babylon was the first king to ever write down rules for his people. His laws told people how to act towards family, land and trade. The law courts were run by ordinary men.

 Show your understanding

1. Look again at the definition of civilisation. What evidence can you find to show that Mesopotamia was a civilised society?
2. List the Mesopotamian inventions which we still use today.
3. Which new Mesopotamian idea do you think has been the most important over time? Write down the idea and explain why you think it is the most important.
4. Imagine you are **curating** a museum exhibit on the new ideas of the Ancient Mesopotamians. What objects would you like to have in your displays? Make a list of at least three objects to tell the story of the developing Mesopotamian civilisation.
5. Your museum is expecting a visit from a group of P6 students. Have a go at either task a) or b).

a) Design a leaflet about the Mesopotamians.
b) Design a poster about the exhibition. Your design should include the following:
   - pictures
   - facts
   - background information
   - an imaginative title

🔍 *Explore further*

Research more about ancient Mesopotamia, looking at areas such as:
- geography
- gods, goddesses, demons and monsters
- Assyrian palaces
- warfare
- Babylon
- the Ziggurats
- astronomers

Who were the ancient Egyptians?

What are we exploring?

By the end of this section you should be able to:

▶ Explain who the ancient Egyptians were
▶ Describe some of the ideas of the ancient Egyptian civilization
▶ Imagine what life was like in ancient Egypt

The Egyptians took many of the new developments from Mesopotamia and added to them. Ancient Egypt had a huge **influence** on the civilisations that developed later, especially the Greeks and Romans. The study of ancient Egypt is called **Egyptology**.

About 5000 years ago, settlers built villages on the banks of the River Nile. Their villages grew into towns and each town was led by a chief. The more powerful chiefs **conquered** their weaker neighbours, and eventually the area was united by force by King Narmer.

A **pharaoh** was a king and a god rolled into one. His job was to watch over the kingdom. When the first pharaohs died they were buried in **Mastabas** – giant mud and brick **tombs**.

⚙ Activate your brain cells!

- In pairs, jot down anything you already know about the Egyptians.
- Volunteer to go to the front and be the expert – tell the class what you know.
- Can the rest of the class add to your ideas?

The oldest stone building in the world!

One pharaoh named Djoser wanted his tomb to be better than those before him. His architect **Imhotep** had the brilliant idea of stacking stones on top of each other, getting smaller and smaller up to the top. In 2611BC Imohtep's builders completed the first pyramid.

The most famous pyramid was built at Giza by the Pharaoh Khuf and is now the world's oldest surviving stone building. It took 100,000 men 20 years to build, moving six million tonnes of stone from up to 500 miles away.

The Egyptians worked out how to **mummify** bodies properly, and believed that when they died they would be able to enter the **afterlife**. Some pharaohs took pets and even servants to the afterlife with them.

What are hieroglyphics?

Egyptian **scribes** wrote down detailed accounts of everyday life. The writing is in the form of **hieroglyphics**, which means 'sacred carvings'. This way of writing used pictures to represent words.

Hieroglyphics can be found on Egyptian buildings and stone tablets like the famous Rosetta Stone, which recorded the **coronation** of Ptolemy V. When Egyptologists worked out the code of the Rosetta Stone in 1822, they were able to better understand Egyptian civilisation as a whole.

The Egyptians also invented **papyrus** by laying strips of **reed-pith** criss-cross on top of each other and pounding them together to make a flat sheet. This was the first time humans had a writing surface that was thin enough to collect together. The Egyptians had invented the book!

What symbols can you see?
What might they mean?

How were Egyptian women treated?

There is evidence to suggest that Egyptian women were not seen as equal to men in all areas of life but they could become **scribes** and **priestesses**, could own property and had good legal rights.

Show your understanding

1. Fill in the missing **consonants** to find the words. There are clues to help you.
   - E __ __ __ __ O __ O G Y (the study of ancient Egypt)
   - N __ R M __ R (pharaoh who united towns to make the kingdom of Egypt)
   - __ A __ __ A __ A___ (tombs made of mud and bricks before pyramids)
   - I __ __ O __ E __ (architect who designed the first pyramid)
   - A __ __ E __ __ I __ E (pharaohs wanted to go here when they died)
2. Make up more puzzles to test your friends. Use any key vocabulary you have learnt so far.
3. Which Egyptian ideas do you think have been the most important for the development of mankind? Explain your answer in detail.
4. Cleopatra is the most famous Egyptian queen in history. Look at Cleopatra's cartouche carefully. (A **cartouche** was the way that Egyptians recognised their leader's writing – a bit like a royal stamp or signature.) What might these symbols mean?
5 Design a cartouche for a friend to show what they are like as a person.

Cleopatra's cartouche

What did ancient Egyptians believe in?

What are we exploring?

By the end of this section you should be able to:

▶ Name some ancient Egyptian gods

▶ Describe what these gods looked like

▶ Imagine why Egyptians believed in these gods

The story of humans is also the story of religion. Understanding what people believe in can help us understand people in the past as well as the present. The ancient Egyptians developed one of the first complex religions.

 Activate your brain cells!

- List the religions you have heard of.
- Why might people believe in these religions? Discuss this with a partner.

Who were the Egyptian gods?

Ra or Amun Re

The most important god in ancient Egypt was **Ra**, the Sun god. He made the Egyptian people, according to their **creation myth**. The Egyptians call themselves the 'Cattle of Ra'. Later, Ra became known as the god **Amun Re**. He controlled the world and everything that happened, and he demanded respect.

Hathor

Cows were important in the Egyptian economy, so the cow-horned goddess Hathor was very popular. The fact that she was also the goddess of music, dancing, happiness and love made her the most popular goddess in Egypt!

Osiris

The son of Amun Re. Egyptians believed that Osiris used his powers to make their crops grow tall and taught the first people to farm. He became King of Earth after Amun Re but was murdered by his brother, **Seth**. Their sister **Isis** embalmed her brother's dead body with the help of **Anubis**. Because Osiris was the first god to die he became the **Lord of the Dead** and the underworld.

Anubis

The jackal-headed god of the dead was the god of **embalming**. He helped make mummies and embalmed the first one ever – Osiris.

Isis

Daughter of Amun Re. The goddess Isis was the protector of women. Egyptians believed her to be a powerful magician. She was the sister of Osiris and was also his wife!

Bes

Bes was the dwarf-god of happiness and the protector of the family. He represented the joys of youth and was a children's entertainer – a kind of scary party-clown! He also married a hippo – literally!

Exploring ancient settlements

20

Sobek

The god of water supplies was thought to control the flow of water in the Nile and the rain in the sky. He had the head of a crocodile and the body of a man.

Thoth

Thoth was the god of truth and wisdom who invented writing, speaking, medicine and mathematics. His job was to write down everything that happened on Earth.

Egyptians believed the Moon to be a wise being that represented truth. Because the Ibis bird has a beak like a crescent Moon, they gave their Moon-god Thoth an Ibis's head.

Seth

Osiris's brother and also his murderer. He was the god of foreign lands, desert storms and chaos. He had a head like an aardvark with a curved snout and square-tipped ears.

Horus

Son of Osiris and Isis. He had the body of a man but the head of a falcon. He looked after pharaohs and was the King of the Living. It was his job to oversee all births. According to myth, he later defeated the evil Seth in a great battle and became King of the Earth.

 Show your understanding

1. Copy and complete a table like the one below. Add your own pictures of the gods.

God	Image	God of...	When ancient Egyptians would pray to this god	Drawing
Amun Re				
Isis				
Osiris				
Horus				
Thoth				
Bes				
Seth				
Sobek				
Hathor				
Anubis				

2. Imagine you are an Egyptian woman in need of help or a farmer in times of drought. Which god would you pray to and why?
3. Explain why the Egyptians worshipped so many Gods.
4. What is troubling you at the moment? Design your own Egyptian god to help you get over this problem.

10 Who were the people of the Indus Valley?

What are we exploring?

By the end of this section you should be able to:

▶ Identify where the ancient Indus Valley civilisation began

▶ Explain the importance of the caste system to Indus Valley civilisation

▶ Imagine life under a caste system in Scotland

Why should I find out about the people of the Indus Valley?

In 1948, the Indus Valley in India was divided into two. Today India and Pakistan are hugely important countries. Together they contain over 1.4 billion people – over 20 per cent of the world's population! India alone is as populous as Europe.

Some Indian communities have changed little – the bullock cart and potter's wheel used in many villages today are identical to those used 4000 years ago. Gods and goddesses from the Stone Age are still worshipped at village shrines.

Four thousand years ago, a civilisation lived in the Indus Valley. It is sometimes called the **Harappan** civilisation after one of its great cities. Archaeologists are finding out more about these people all the time.

 Activate your brain cells!

- Do you know what you want to do when you leave school? Create a list of jobs your class would like to do.
- How would you feel if you were told you could not do these jobs but would always be a street-sweeper instead?

Another site in Pakistan at **Mohenjo-Daro** is being excavated today. These two great cities each had up to 33,000 people living in them – that is about the same size as the population of Stirling. The people were given rules to lead their lives by. Knowledge and new ideas were encouraged.

Buildings in these cities were complex and sometimes more than one storey high. Streets were in a grid system like Glasgow or modern American cities. Houses were protected from noise, smells and thieves.

They had **drainage systems** and lots of areas for washing, which is still an important **ritual** in the Hindu religion. They were the first civilisation to grow cotton and make clothes from it. They used this cotton to **trade** overseas.

The Indus civilisation was the first to develop a precise system of **weights** and **measures**.

They worked out new techniques in using metals, and produced copper, bronze, lead and tin. They were especially good at engineering, for example building docks after careful studying of tides, waves and currents.

What is the caste system?

The tribes of the Indus Valley divided their people into different classes according to their jobs. Children belonged to the same class as their parents and everyone knew their place and what job they had to do. They could **never** change jobs. This way of grouping people together was known as the **caste system**.

The caste system still exists in parts of modern India and Pakistan and affects the lives of millions of people.

 **Show your understanding**

1. Here are the four original caste groups in Indus Valley civilisation. Arrange them in the order you think would have been most important to the people at the time. Which caste do you think the majority of people belonged to?
    Merchants and farmers
    Workers
    Warriors and kings
    Priests and scholars
2. Choose either a) or b).
    a) Draw a diagram with lots of figures like the ones here. Organise the figures according to what jobs they do by using different colours. Label the groups with the title of their job.
       • Why is this a good system for getting things done in a civilisation?
       • What problems can you find with this system of organising?
    b) Imagine you live in a society that follows the caste system. Write a letter to a friend explaining what the caste system is and how you feel about your future as a result of it.

📁 **Collect a skill**

History is science too!

Archaeologists exploring Mohenjo-Daro asked many scientists to help them investigate. Work with a friend to match the method used to the type of information found. Which scientific skill would you like to specialise in?

What you would use	If you wanted to find out...
Osteology: Measuring the shape and size of human bones	A. The types of meat people ate
Pollen analysis: Using a microscope to identify different types of pollen from plants	B. The age of an organic object such as a piece of wood
Biology: Examining animal bones	C. The sex, age and health of a buried person
Geophysics: Passing an electrical current through the ground; stone gives a different signal from soil	D. How big a settlement was
Radiocarbon dating: Measuring how much carbon-14 is left in once-living things and working out how old they are	E. The type of crops farmers grew
Ground survey: Counting the number of objects found in a set area	F. Finding walls buried under the ground

11 Why was ancient China so powerful?

What are we exploring?

By the end of this section you should be able to:

▶ Explain how the silk road made China powerful
▶ Describe some of the main features of ancient Chinese society
▶ Compare ancient China with other ancient civilisations

The history of China is very different from that of the '**western world**'. The way of life that developed there was unlike anywhere else in the ancient world and its early history is filled with myths and legends.

People began to set up farms along the Yellow River around 5000BC. They farmed a type of grain called millet as well as vegetables, nuts and fruit. Some kept pigs, dogs and chickens. At the same time, along the Yangtze River, people grew rice because the weather was warmer and wetter.

Chinese **merchants** took their goods, including silk, gold and iron ore, further west. The route they took became known as the '**silk road**'. Silk was very popular in the west, but the Chinese merchants refused to reveal the secret of how it was made.

 Activate your brain cells!

● What do you know already about Chinese society? Make a list in groups.
● Can you find China in an atlas? How large is China compared to the following: Britain, USA, France, Russia, Egypt?
● Does it have any natural features like rivers, mountains or coastlines?

Once the Chinese merchants sold their goods, they returned to China with furs, precious stones, glass, pearls, ivory, donkeys and even camels! China became a powerful economic civilisation.

The following are all Chinese inventions:

● gunpowder
● water pumps
● silk looms
● paper
● simple **seismograph** (which measured earthquakes using water).

As their civilisation developed, Chinese thinkers made great progress in these four areas of knowledge. Which one do you think is the most important?

● astronomy
● maths
● using herbs in medicine
● using acupuncture in medicine.

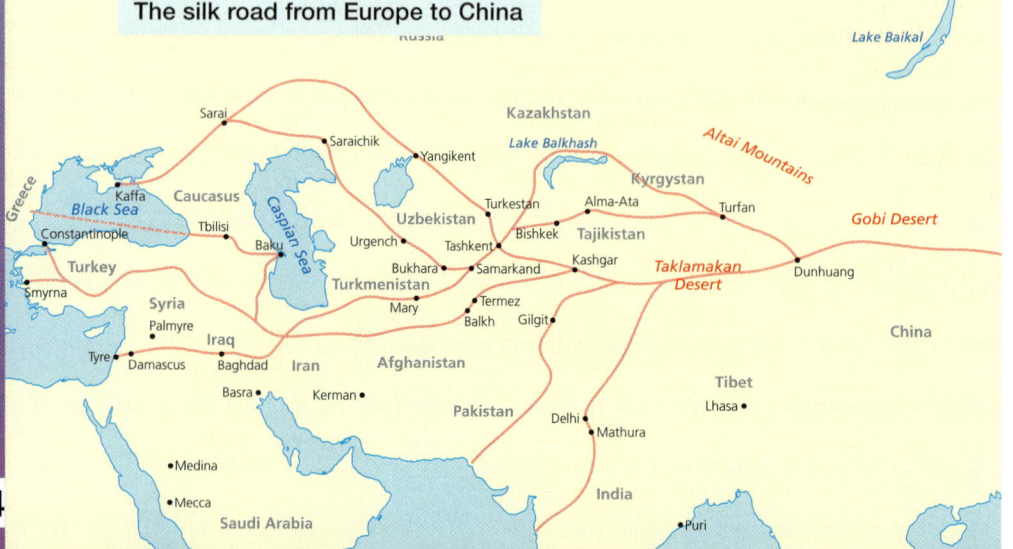
The silk road from Europe to China

Smart thinkers

Philosophy means thinking about your way of life. Ancient China had many philosophers. In 600BC Lao Tzu founded the philosophy of **Taoism**, which said that people should try to live in harmony with the Universe. Instead of living by rigid rules and laws, people should try to work with the natural way of the world, and in this way their lives would be easier and happier.

About 50 years later, Confucius came along and disagreed with Lao Tzu. Confucius taught that people should recognise their responsibilities and work to uphold the laws and customs of their society. If everyone was a good citizen, the whole community would benefit and everyone would be happier.

You can see that these two ideas conflict with each other. Yet both Taoism and **Confucianism** were popular all over China for the next 2000 years, and they are still both popular today.

 Show your understanding

1. How did the act of selling silk make China powerful? Discuss with a partner.
2. Sketch a map of the silk road. Label your map with brief sentences, highlighting the most important events of the journey.
3. What evidence can you find that this civilisation was inventive?
4. What evidence can you find to suggest that this civilisation valued knowledge?
5. In pairs, pretend to be either Lao Tzu or Confucius. Explain why your philosophy is the correct way for people to lead their lives. Try to come up with ideas for and against both philosophies.
6. Hold a class debate about Taoism and Confucianism.

🔍 *Explore further*

1. Compare the four civilisations you have explored so far by completing the table below.
2. You run a time-travel company! Design a poster advertising a trip to one of the four civilisations you have explored so far. Include the following:

   - pictures
   - price
   - information on what the travellers on your trip will see
   - an eye-catching title

The Chinese philosopher Confucius

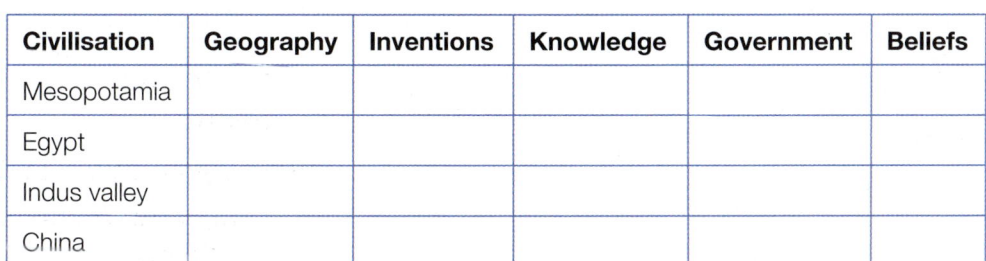

Civilisation	Geography	Inventions	Knowledge	Government	Beliefs
Mesopotamia					
Egypt					
Indus valley					
China					

12 How did the Athenians invent politics?

By the end of this section you should be able to:

▶ Explain what democracy means
▶ Compare democracy in Athens with Scotland today
▶ Use secondary sources to help you come to a conclusion

In a **democracy**, every adult has the right to vote. Whatever most people vote for is the course of action taken by the country. This way of organising society was first tried in ancient Greece. In Greek, the word democracy means 'the rule of the people'.

The first people to try and rule the whole area were the **Mycenaeans**, who brutally attacked other cities in Greece. Legend has it that in 1184BC their king Agamemnon captured the Greek city of Troy.

Hundreds of years later, poets telling the story of Troy added myths such as gods, heroes and the famous wooden horse! In 850BC these stories were collected by **Homer** in his books *The Iliad* and *The Odyssey*.

 Activate your brain cells!

- Have a class vote on which of the two tasks below your class should try.
  1. Who should run the country? Make a list of five people you think would do a good job!
  2. Imagine if you ran Scotland; what would be your first new rule?
- Which task did you choose? Were there any disagreements? Would this be a good way to start every lesson?

Greece is a very mountainous land with lots of small islands in the Mediterranean Sea. Why would this make ruling the whole area difficult?

The Greek area became a collection of independent **city-states** rather than one large country. These city-states spent a lot of time fighting each other. Over time, two city-states became the most powerful: Athens and Sparta.

Athens was known for its ideas and culture: poetry, music, dance, books and drama. Sparta was known for its fierce warriors!

What was this first democracy like?

In 508BC the people of Athens replaced their leader and became the first democracy in the world. Laws were decided by male citizens over the age of 30 at a regular meeting called an **assembly**. Women, foreigners, slaves and the poor were not allowed.

Most men couldn't always vote because they had work to do, such as planting their grain and fighting wars. Only a few men were chosen to do most of the voting. The rest only joined in when there was a really important vote.

Athens chose these assembly members in a lottery. If you got the winning ticket then you were on the **council** of 500 men and would serve for a year.

SOURCE A – FROM A DISCUSSION ON WWW.ANCIENTGREECE.CO.UK

'The Athenians were **hypocrites**. On the one hand they wanted democracy to give people more freedom but on the other they had slaves.'

SOURCE B – FROM A BOOK ON ANCIENT ATHENS

'The Athenians should not be criticised too harshly for the fact they had slaves. At the time, every ancient civilisation accepted slavery and saw no reason why it should stop... Greek city-states made money from the slave trade by creating slaves from those they defeated in war.'

Show your understanding

1. Write a sentence or two to describe the word democracy.
2. Copy this diagram, showing who could and could not vote in Athens.

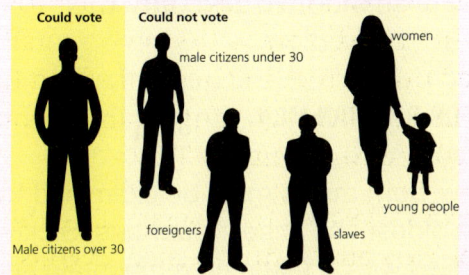

With a partner, create a similar diagram for who can vote in Scotland today.
3. Which society do you think is more democratic? Why?

Collect a skill

Using sources to come to a conclusion
Historians love to argue and debate issues. Here are two secondary sources about democracy in Athens.

1. What reason does **Source A** give to suggest Athens did not have a real democracy?
2. What argument does **Source B** use to disagree with what **Source A** says?
3. Do you think ancient Athens was as democratic as Scotland is today? Use the sources and what you have read to help you write your answer.

13 What was the Spartan experiment?

What are we exploring?

By the end of this section you should be able to:

▶ Describe how Spartan life was organised

▶ Explain the reasons why it was organised in this way

▶ Imagine what it would be like to live in Sparta

The rules for people in the ancient Greek city-state of Sparta were very different from the democratic ideas of Athens. The word '**spartan**' is used today to describe a lifestyle that is very simple, strict and without luxuries. Spartan rules aimed to create a mighty and pure society where the weak were abandoned and only the strongest survived!

 Activate your brain cells!

- What behaviours disrupt lessons? With a partner, make a list of rules that would stop the bad behaviour.
- Compare your rules with the rest of the class. Are all these rules fair?
- Why do we have rules and who should decide what they are?

RULES FOR SPARTAN MEN

- New-born males must be examined by the oldest and wisest Spartans. Sickly babies will be taken up a mountain and left to die.
- All boys begin military training at the age of seven to learn how to become fearless warriors.
- Boys must steal their own food. They are punished if they are caught – not for stealing but for being clumsy enough to have been found out!
- Men must have no money or comforts. They must all dress the same and eat together in big halls.
- No culture. Art, music and books are forbidden.
- Men must obey strict military discipline. Spartan **Hoplite** soldiers are expected to defend their city first, not their families.

- Hoplites are trained to organise themselves into a **phalanx**. A rectangular formation of closely locked men, shields and spears.
- The phalanx depends on all men working together. One drooping shield will end in failure and death.
- Before battle, Hoplites are to prepare by calmly combing their hair and oiling their bodies.
- A Hoplite returning from battle without his shield will be sentenced to death for failing.
- The very best soldiers are rewarded with the opportunity to breed with up to twenty Spartan women. It is hoped that any resulting children will have their father's strength and abilities.
- Once married, a couple must not live together. The man must continue to live with his fellow soldiers.

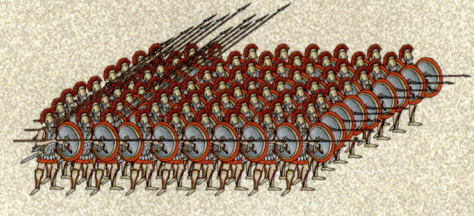

What happened at Thermopylae?

In 490BC, a Persian king called Darius demanded that Greek city-states surrender to him. Athens and Sparta refused and teamed up to defeat the Persians at the Battle of **Marathon**.

In 480BC a huge Persian army came back for a rematch. The battle site at Thermopylae was a narrow pass between the sea and the cliffs. It was defended by just 300 Spartans led by their king, Leonidas.

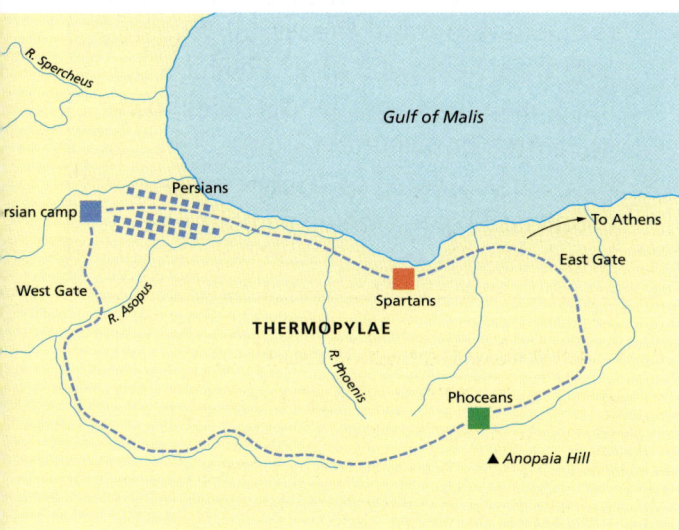

At first the Spartans fought off huge numbers of Persians, but a Greek traitor showed the Persians a secret path through the mountains. The Persians used this to creep up behind the Spartans and **ambush** them. Leonidas and his men stayed until the last of them died, making this battle famous for showing the courage of the Spartan way of life.

? Bore your friends...

Adolf Hitler was so impressed by Spartan ideas that he created the Hitler Youth movement in Germany in the 1930s. Child members were taught that their duty to their country was more important than their families.

SPARTAN RULES FOR WOMEN

- A Spartan woman has to be beautiful, intelligent and strong so that her children are also these things.
- When a woman marries her hair will be cropped and she must dress as a boy.
- Weak women must not get married and should be cast out of society.

🧩 Show your understanding

1. Which of these words could be used to describe Spartan society?
   fair strict proud sexist military unorganised relaxed cultured
2. Sketch the map of the Battle of Thermopylae. Label your map with brief sentences highlighting the most important events of the battle.
3. With a partner, discuss what the term '**selective breeding**' could mean. Ask your Biology teacher about selective breeding in plants and animals. How similar is Spartan society to the scientific idea of selective breeding?
4. Choose to answer either a) or b).
   a) Imagine you are Leonidas, king of the Spartans. Design an illustrated handbook for Spartan men describing all the rules.
   b) Imagine you are a Spartan wife. Write a letter to your Athenian cousin describing the different lifestyles of the two city-states. Which do you prefer and why?

14 What was so great about Alexander?

What are we exploring?

By the end of this section you should be able to:

▶ Define what the word **empire** means
▶ Describe how the past is organised
▶ Explain why people call him 'Alexander the Great'

An **empire** is created when one country takes over the land of another country and controls it. You will explore other empires in this book, so we should look closely at this idea.

Study this map. It shows all the countries controlled by King Alexander of Macedonia in 323BC. Which countries do you recognise the names of? What do you know about these countries?

 Activate your brain cells!

• Imagine you and your partner could take over a third of the world! Which countries would you pick? Collect a blank map from your teacher and colour in an area or a country.

• How are you going to control these countries? What problems might you have?

In 336BC, a 20 year-old Alexander became King of Macedonia and northern Greece. He wanted to see the world. He was inspired by his favourite book, Homer's **The Illiad**, and by his teacher, the great philosopher **Aristotle**. He did not simply want to see the places he visited; he wanted to own them! He wanted his own **empire**.

For the next 14 years, Alexander led an army of 42,000 Greek soldiers through Persia, Egypt and even as far as India. He was made pharaoh in Egypt and had 70 new cities named after him, including **Alexandria** in Egypt.

Alexander's march into India was a step too far for his soldiers, who made him turn back because they had had enough after eight years of moving and fighting and were homesick. By the time he died of mysterious poisoning in 323BC, Alexander owned the largest empire the world had ever seen.

How did Alexander keep control of all these people?

What did the creator of this mosaic of Alexander think of him?

Alexander made sure his **empire** was run by people from Persia, not just his own countrymen.

Alexander made sure people spoke Greek across all his lands.

He made many of his former soldiers live as leaders in his new lands. This helped to control his empire and prevent **rebellion**.

Thousands of Greek people, soldiers, merchants, artists, scientists and thinkers moved around the empire and spread their ideas.

Alexander married a Persian princess. He also organised a huge wedding for 9000 of his soldiers to marry women from the lands he conquered.

Alexander was seen as the greatest Greek hero by the Romans. They used him as a heroic example when they sought to create their own empire.

The famous library at Alexandria contained copies of all the known books in the world. People came to Alexandria all the time to study Greek ideas.

Alexander's empire became very rich.

Trade between Greece and the rest of Alexander's empire continued long after his death.

His leaders upheld Greek laws and lived in Greek-style houses, even though they were not in Greece.

Show your understanding

1. Write a sentence or two describing the word 'empire'.
2. How did Alexander keep **control** of his empire? Write down the three most important facts from the list. Give reasons for your choices.
3. Complete either task a) or b).
   a) Design a poster for a new movie about the life of Alexander.
   b) Record a podcast trailer for a movie about Alexander the Great.

For both tasks, you should include details about how Alexander kept control of his empire.

'Veni, vidi, vici': who came, who saw, who conquered?

The birth of democracy

What are we exploring?

By the end of this section you should be able to:

▶ Explain why the Roman army was so powerful

▶ Describe how ancient Roman society was organised

▶ Imagine what life was like in ancient Rome

Activate your brain cells!

- All the things in this cartoon were brought to Britain by the Romans. How many can you name?
- If someone said 'The Romans were just brutal empire builders. What did they ever do for us?' how might you begin to answer them?

Public Library

Heated Public Baths

The Roman Empire in AD 180

From 27BC, the **emperors** of Rome controlled a growing empire. Julius Caesar bragged '*Veni, vidi, vici*', which translates from **Latin** into 'I came, I saw, I conquered'. At its largest size, the Roman Empire covered much of Europe, North Africa and the Near East.

Why was the army successful?

Romans admired the way the Spartan army was organised. Young Romans were told to put the 'Glory of Rome' above family and friends. The Roman army was the fittest, most disciplined and best equipped army in the world.

A professional Roman **legionary** soldier joined up for 25 years and had tough training. He was paid good wages and became highly skilled at fighting battles and laying **siege** to enemy camps. One tactic was for soldiers to huddle together and make a tortoise-like defence with their shields. Soldiers were also trained as **engineers**. They set up temporary camps with ditches, fences and even toilets – the remains of these can be found all over Europe.

Roman armies built larger forts in areas where they wanted to protect the land they had gained. These forts could hold up to 500 men. Several cities in Europe grew up around these forts. In fact the word **chester** was the Roman word for a settlement.

Soldiers from defeated armies were encouraged to join the Roman army. These **auxiliary** soldiers were specialist fighters such as cavalrymen, archers and slingers.

How was society organised?

Rich male citizens had special rights and showed their importance by wearing **togas**. They could vote in elections and serve in the army. The poor citizens or **plebeians** worked as farmers, shopkeepers or craft workers. They could also vote.

The people with the least power were women, slaves and people in Roman-controlled **provinces**. These people could get citizenship by working hard and being loyal to Rome.

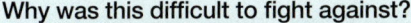

Why was this difficult to fight against?

Show your understanding

1. Copy the following sentences and mark if they are true or false. If you believe the sentence is false, write the correct sentence underneath.
   - Emperors used war to boost their popularity and authority.
   - The Roman army executed all armies they defeated.
   - Women in Rome had few rights unless they were given special citizenship for working hard.
   - People in the provinces had the same power as the citizens of Rome.
2. You are a **Barbarian** spy! Ask the person next to you about the strengths of the Roman army. Now write a secret report to your leader telling him why you think the Roman army will be difficult to defeat.

Collect a skill

Arranging time

Visual timelines are a good way to organise what happened and when. How does this timeline help you understand the connections between ancient civilisations?

Copy the timeline below and complete it by filling in the boxes with the correct information from below and adding illustrations.

- The Roman Empire lasted from **around** 27BC until AD395.
- The ancient Greek city-states lasted from **about** 1100BC until 50BC.
- The Egyptian Empire lasted from **approximately** 3100BC until 27BC.
- Alexander the Great's Empire lasted from *circa* 336BC until 100BC.

Any of the words in bold can be used when historians cannot decide on an exact date.

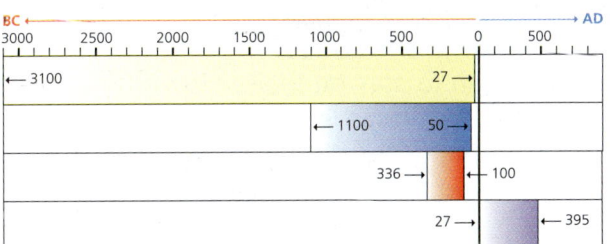

A timeline for ancient civilisations

16 How does an empire control its people?

When the powerful Roman army marched into a defeated land, hardly anybody resisted. Most people in the provinces preferred to be ruled by the Romans. The Roman army protected them from the brutal Barbarian tribes of northern Europe. It was also a chance to get money and power by becoming like the Romans. This was called **Romanisation**.

Activate your brain cells!

• Have you ever copied someone? It could be a hairstyle, an answer, an idea or an action. Think hard and be honest! Share it with the person next to you.

• What makes people follow others? Try to come up with as many reasons as you can.

SOURCE A – TACITUS, WRITING ABOUT HIS FATHER-IN-LAW

Before we Romans came, the Britons were a filthy and dull people. So Governor Agricola wanted to give the Britons a taste of Mediterranean luxury. He helped them build town squares, baths and town-houses in a Roman style. He gave sons of rich locals an education. Soon they became keen to speak Latin well and the toga was everywhere to be seen. The Britons described these things as civilised and hoped to become citizens of Rome themselves.

It was wise to encourage Romanisation. Instead of guarding their good ideas and wealth, the Romans were ready to share them. By making people want to respect and obey Rome, the emperors were able to control their vast empire.

Local official

Julius Caesar has given us a proper calendar so that there are 12 months and 365 days in the year. This calendar has made organising things so much easier. I've started writing in Latin so that I'll be able to communicate with Rome as well as the rich people here – it's the language of the future!

Rich landowner

Emperor Claudius' army arrived in Britain in AD43. I was keen to stay on their side from the start. Now they have let me keep my land and I've become richer by selling grain to the soldiers in the nearby fort. I've also been able to build my own villa like the ones in Rome.

Queen Boudicca

I am queen of the Iceni tribe and I am furious. When the brutal Romans arrived I was flogged and my daughters were assaulted. The Romans demand taxes from us – who are they to take our money and freedom? My revenge will be fierce and bloody – I have 120,000 tribesmen to command. We have wiped out the Roman Ninth Legion at Colchester and are now going to burn London down to the ground!

 ## Show your understanding

1. Write a sentence or two to explain what the idea of Romanisation was.
2. According to Source A, how were people encouraged to be like the Romans?
3. The year is AD84. Imagine Scotland has been invaded by the Romans! List reasons for and against fighting them, using the arguments in the text to help you. Then have a vote to see what everyone would do.

Reasons I should fight the Romans	Reasons I should become like the Romans

4. What evidence can you find that some things and people were not fully Romanised?

 ## Collect a skill

Wrestle with Roman numerals!

Getting everyone to use their numbering system helped the Romans control the empire. Merchants had to understand the Roman way of writing numbers to know how much they were buying and selling.

You can still see lots of Roman numerals in use today. Next time you watch a TV programme look at the end of the credits to find out if the date is written in Roman numerals. Can you think of anywhere else Roman numerals are used?

1. Copy the table and fill in the blanks.
2. Now try the following maths questions:
   a) V + VI   =   **d)** XIX – IV   =
   b) VI + IX =   **e)** V x II   =
   c) X – IV   =
3. The number 185 would look like this:
   CLXXXV because C = 100, L = 50, X = 10 (times 3 = 30), and V = 5.
   Try to work out what these dates would be in Roman numerals: 300, 990, 1066, 2010.

Arabic numeral	Roman numeral
1	I
2	II
3	
4	IV
5	V
6	
7	VII
8	
9	IX
10	X
11	
50	L
100	C
500	D
1000	M

17 Why did the Romans build walls?

What are we exploring?

By the end of this section you should be able to:

▶ Explain why Hadrian's Wall and the Antonine Wall were built

▶ Describe the relationship between Romans and locals

▶ Imagine what life around Hadrian's wall would have been like

After invading southern Britain in AD43, the army of Governor Agricola pushed north towards what we now call Scotland. Some tribal chiefs in the south made peace rather than fight against them, but the **Caledonians** of the north, led by **Calgacus**, refused to make peace.

In AD84 the legions defeated the Caledonians at the battle of Mons Graupius. Calgacus's troops fled to the northern hills to recover strength. The Romans found it impossible to crush these troops and the other tribes who refused to make peace.

In AD122 Emperor Hadrian ordered a wall to be put across the country. He wanted to control the movement of tribes and trading across the border and mark the limit of his empire. It also made him look powerful. The modern border between Scotland and England runs close to the line of Hadrian's Wall.

Hadrian's Wall

- took six years to build
- was 72 miles long, from Tyne to Solway
- was five metres high, three metres thick and had a steep ditch on the Caledonian side (about nine metres wide and four metres deep)
- every mile there were gates through the wall, defended by a castle and manned by 30 soldiers

Activate your brain cells!

- Why do people build walls? Try to come up with as many purposes as you can.
- Can you name any famous walls in the world? What were these built for?

- 16 forts were built along the wall to house between 500 and 1000 men, they contained stores and a hospital and bath houses were built outside for the soldiers to relax in
- settlements grew up around the forts
- locals traded with the soldiers and earned Roman gold for their cloth, beer, leather, wheat, barley, pots, bedding and other goods
- the **Vindolanda tablets** give us good evidence about what life was like on the wall

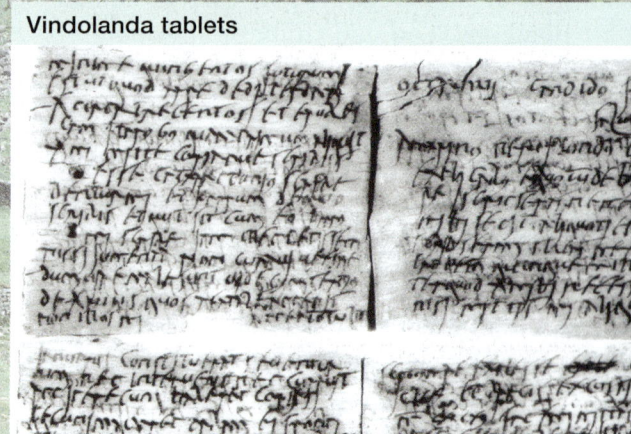

Vindolanda tablets

The Antonine Wall

The Roman army entered the far north of modern Scotland at least four more times to try and defeat the northern tribes. Archaeologists have found more Roman marching camps in northern Scotland than anywhere else in Europe!

The Antonine Wall was built in AD142 and ran for 38 miles along the Forth and Clyde line. It was a turf wall with high sharp stakes on top. At regular points there were platforms with fire beacons on them, ready to send signals along the wall if Caledonians attacked.

The Antonine Wall lasted for just 20 years. The Roman army seems to have retreated back to Hadrian's Wall. Perhaps the area was peaceful, or maybe the Caledonians attacked and pushed the Roman army back.

How did the Roman Empire fall?

The empire controlled a huge area. Historians think it became too expensive and difficult to defend it. After AD180, the empire began to weaken badly. In AD367 Picts from the north smashed through Hadrian's Wall and raided deep into southern Britain. Similar events happened all over the empire.

By AD395 the empire was divided in two – a western and an eastern empire. In AD410 Rome itself was invaded and almost destroyed by the **Visigoth** tribes. The German **Goths** finally took over in AD476.

Emperor **Constantine** had already moved his capital east to Constantinople in modern-day Turkey (the city is now called Istanbul). From there the emperors continued to rule what was left of the eastern Roman Empire.

Show your understanding

1. Sketch a map of Scotland in AD142 showing both walls.
2. Why was Hadrian's Wall built? Find four reasons.
3. Put this sequence of events in the right order. Add the date when these events happened:
   - the Antonine Wall was built
   - the Roman Empire fell apart
   - Picts smashed through Hadrian's Wall
   - the Caledonians were defeated at Mons Graupius
   - Rome was invaded by the Visigoths
   - Hadrian's Wall was built
4. Write a short paragraph explaining how and why the Roman Empire fell apart.
5. Ask the person next to you to write down two good points and one bad point about your paragraph. How could your written answers be improved?

Explore further

Research more about areas of the ancient Roman world such as:
- Emperors
- Gods and goddesses
- Roman buildings
- Weapons and warfare
- Hannibal and his elephants
- Slaves and gladiators

18 Why do people move from place to place?

By the end of this section you should be able to:

▶ Explain why people have moved from place to place

▶ Describe what different Celtic settlements looked like

▶ Imagine living in a Celtic settlement

Activate your brain cells!

- Have you always lived in the house you live in now?
- How many people in the class have lived in more than one place?
- What reasons might force or attract people to move?

Who were the Celts?

You may have heard people describe Ireland, Scotland, Wales, Cornwall, and even parts of France and Spain as '**Celtic**' nations.

The Celts were a very important group of tribes in Europe from 700BC to around AD446. The early Celts began in Germany, Austria and parts of France. They traded in the metals everyone wanted – copper and iron ore. They were strong, horse-riding warriors. When they fought and defeated

their neighbours, they took animals, goods and riches as their prize.

From 700BC many Celtic tribes began to leave their homes, running from wars with other Celtic tribes and from the spread of the Roman Empire. Some historians think of them as **cowboys**, settling on the land, taking what they needed, fighting the locals, sometimes marrying them or moving on.

Because many Scottish tribes, such as the Picts, **descended** from them it is important to understand what they were like.

SOURCE A – from the Roman historian Tacitus, writing in 100BC

'The Celts are barbarians. Their hair is stiff and pale because they cover it in chalk when wet. They are tall, well-built, fierce warriors. They worship strange gods and their **druid** priests violently sacrifice their own people. Rome must defeat them.'

What were their settlements like?

Round house

This had a simple wooden frame and a **thatched** roof. Walls were made of woven sticks covered in a sticky mixture of mud and straw. This would stop the wind and rain getting in. A **hearth** in the middle of the roundhouse would keep a family warm in winter, and their animals stayed with them at night for extra warmth.

Broch

Brochs were high, round stone towers found on farmland next to the coast. Some were as tall as 15 metres. Historians have different ideas about what they were used for. Some think that their size and strength means that they were used to defend families from attack. Others think that brochs were more likely used to protect a family's valuable things like cattle or grain, rather than the people themselves. Brochs are found only in Scotland. There are over 100 sites, including the famous Mousa broch in Shetland.

Crannog

Roundhouses were sometimes built on stilts above the water of lochs or marshes. Archaeologists have built a crannog at Loch Tay in Perthshire to show us what the settlement would have looked like. Beneath the crannog, in the water, are **middens**. These provide lots of evidence about the types of food settlers ate, such as fish, grain and berries. Historians cannot decide why crannogs were built on water. Some think that it was for defence. The wooden bridge to the shore could be destroyed easily in times of trouble and prevent enemies reaching the settlers. Crannogs were common in Scotland – over 600 have been discovered so far.

Hill fort

Forts were built high on hilltops to help defend settlers in times of attack. They had thick stone walls following the shape of the hill and sometimes had ditches outside them. One of the largest hill forts was discovered at Eildon Hill in the Scottish Borders. At one time it held up to 3000 people. Historians think that the settlements nearby may have only used the fort in times of trouble.

 Show your understanding

1. Write a sentence or two to explain what made the Celts move to Scotland.
2. What might the term 'Celtic cowboy' mean?
3. Copy and complete the table below.

Type of settlement	Why was it built?	Main features
Round house		
Broch		
Crannog		
Hill fort		

4. In a group, plan a model of one of the four settlements. Make a list of the materials you would need to build it. Give each other job titles and assign tasks.

19 How have the Picts been pictured?

What are we exploring?

By the end of this section you should be able to:

▶ Explain where and when the Picts lived

▶ Identify different ideas about what Pictish people were like

▶ Explain to another person what you think the truth is about the Picts

Activate your brain cells!

- As a class, arrange yourselves in a circle. One person whispers a sentence about the Celts into the ear of the person next to them and so on.
- The last person has to say out loud what they think the sentence was.
- Did the sentence change? Who changed it and why?
- Why should we try to find out the truth about people and events? Discuss with a partner.

Old history books described the Picts as violent, tattooed warriors who fought the Romans north of Hadrian's Wall. The word Pict was thought to mean 'painted people'.

In 1800, Sir Walter Scott wrote that they were actually small people who could fit through the small door of the broch where they lived. In 1900, John Buchan wrote a short story about the 'troll-like' Picts of Galloway. In fact there is no evidence that any of this is true!

We actually know very little about the **Pictish** people. What has been found by archaeologists can fill in only a few of the gaps in our knowledge.

What do we know for sure about the Picts?

The Picts lived in the north and east of Scotland between AD200 and AD900. They were descended from Celtic settlers and had sorted themselves into seven tribal kingdoms, led by chieftains.

The name Pict probably does not come from the term 'painted people'. Modern historians think that the name comes from the ancient Celtic word *'pett'* or pit, which means 'a piece of land'. This word appears in many place names in areas where Pictish tribes settled.

The Picts were good farmers, skilled craftspeople and metalworkers. Archaeologists have **unearthed** jewels made from silver and gold and mysterious pictures of animals, important objects and battle scenes that were carved into huge stone slabs. Many stones have **Ogham** symbol carvings. This is an ancient alphabet used in Celtic societies.

Could this be what picts looked like?

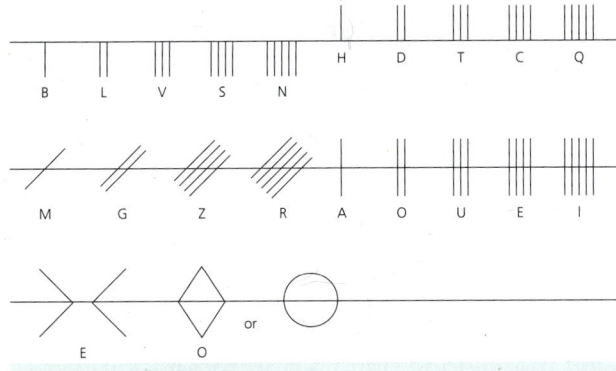

The Ogham alphabet

The **Aberlemno stone** tells the story of the battle of Nechtansmere in AD685, when King Bridei led his Picts to victory against raiders from Northumbria. Some historians think this is the most important battle in Scotland's history. The Picts fought off the invading Angles and made sure that most of Scotland's tribes kept their freedom. If the Picts had lost, Scotland might never have existed.

Where did the Picts go?

The only Pictish piece of writing we have is a list of their kings. Mysteriously, the list stops suddenly with the death of King Causantin mac Cinaeda in AD876.

Yet the Picts didn't just disappear: they joined the mix of populations and tribes that eventually led to the formation of modern Scotland.

The Aberlemno stone

Show your understanding

1. Copy the following sentences and mark whether they are true or false. If you believe the sentence is false, explain why.
   * the Picts were really small people
   * the Picts were skilled metalworkers
   * the Picts were fierce warriors
   * the name Pict comes from the fact they painted pictures on themselves
   * the Pictish army saved Scotland by winning the battle of Nechtansmere
2. With a partner, study a map of Scotland. Find as many places beginning with 'Pit' or 'Pet' as you can. Why are there so many?
3. Look at the Aberlemno stone. In pairs, discuss the following:
   * One warrior is chasing another who has thrown his sword and shield away. Which one do you think is a Pict?
   * Two enemies are seen fighting on horseback. Why do you think the large raven is shown?
   * Why is this primary source important for the history of Scotland?
   * Compare your ideas with another pair, and then the rest of the class.
4. Complete either a) or b).
   a) design your own Pictish symbol
   b) draw a line and write your own name in the Ogham alphabet along it.

Collect a skill

The importance of truth

Often in History we have to look past myths and legends to find the truth. The Picts are a good example of this.

1. Search for 'spoof websites' and have a look at a few appropriate ones. Think about blogs, emails and websites.
2. Why should we be careful about what we read on the Internet? Where else can you find out reliable information?

20 Were the Vikings all that bad?

 Activate your brain cells!

- Sit back to back in a pair.
- Describe what you think a **Viking** looks like whilst your partner draws your description. Does it look like the Viking you had in your head?
- What problems did you have with this task? What skills did you use during it?

Who were the Vikings?

The Vikings came from Norway, Denmark and Sweden, they travelled to **raid** other lands or trade with the people. Sometimes they settled beside or within other communities. Many had settled in Orkney, Shetland and northern Scotland by AD800.

Older History books describe the Vikings as ferocious warriors: murdering, stealing, raping and pillaging. How true is this?

→ Viking journeys, 8th–11th centuries

The Vikings travelled across the globe

Source A

Fierce warriors sailed ashore to steal all they could. They seized animals, food, tools, weapons, precious metals and jewellery and sometimes took women as slaves. They fought their way around the coast and sometimes up rivers, raiding villages and towns as they went.

Source B

The **Norsemen** set out from Norway to look for more food to feed their growing population. Scandinavian land and weather were very poor. The Vikings could not grow enough crops to supply their people's needs. They had to turn to raiding other lands to survive.

Source C

Vikings were often accepted peacefully by people in northern Scotland. There is little evidence of battles between the Picts and the Vikings.

Source D

Vikings were daring and determined **explorers**. One leader, Eric the Red, explored huge parts of Greenland and his son Leif Ericson reached the Americas. The Vikings' ability to travel and trade took some as far east as Baghdad. They sold swords and walrus tusks to Muslims in return for silks, precious stones and gold.

Source E

Viking stories suggest that the first Vikings raiders in Scotland were **outlaws**. These outcasts may have sailed to Scotland to escape punishment and continue their vicious thieving, slaving and murdering. It is possible that these Norsemen have given the rest a bad name. Most Norwegian farmers were probably law-abiding people and did not go on the first Viking raids.

Source F

The main evidence for the terrifying behaviour of the Vikings comes from the pens of churchmen. They were appalled by the raids on churches and monasteries. They describe the Vikings as brutal and vicious. Vikings were **pagans** who worshipped violent gods like **Thor**, the hammer-holding god of thunder, and **Odin**, the warrior god. They had no fear of destroying and stealing gold objects from the poorly defended churches.

Source G

When the rich monastery at Lindisfarne in northern England was attacked in AD793, all of Christian Europe was shocked. Important cities such as Paris, Seville and Pisa were attacked. Vikings had become the professional pirates of Europe.

Source H

Viking warriors are usually shown wearing frightening-looking helmets with animal horns stuck on. In fact, these were only worn for ceremonies or religious occasions. The normal helmets had no horns. They sometimes had a nose-plate, an eye-guard and a **chain-mail** neck guard for protection.'

Show your understanding

1. a) Split into groups of three to create a news report describing what Vikings were really like.
   Expert: it is your job to read up on the topic.
   Reporter and **newsreader**: prepare interview questions to ask the expert.
   b) The reporter interviews the expert on the reputation of the Vikings.
   c) The newsreader records the answers and creates a 60-second news flash.
   d) The newsreader delivers the news flash to the group.
2. Choose to answer either a) or b).
   a) Write a script for a film about the Vikings.
   • List the characters and briefly write down what the key scenes will be.
   • Convince your movie producer partner that your script is worth investing in!
   b) Write a paragraph explaining why the traditional idea of the Vikings as murderous thieves is not necessarily true.

? Bore your friends...

The Viking epic poem Beowulf *is seen as one of the most important stories of European history. The hero Beowulf battles a monster called Grendel, who has been attacking the Viking warriors in Denmark. Grendel's witch mother and her dragon also fight the hero.*

A Viking raid on a village

21 How was 'Scotland' born?

What are we exploring?

By the end of this section you should be able to:

▶ Explain what Scottish heritage is

▶ Describe how the Picts and the Scots united into one nation

▶ Think about why this event was so important for Scotland's history

Where does Scotland's heritage begin?

Before AD843, the idea of 'Scotland' did not exist. After the Romans left in AD411, four **kingdoms** held power:

- The **Picts** covered northern Scotland from the River Forth to Shetland.
- The **Britons** held Dumbarton Rock and the south. They wrote using an Old Welsh Celtic language.
- The **Gaels** or Gaelic-speaking people of **Dál Riata** had their royal fortress at Dunadd in Argyll. Their descendants may have originally come from Ireland. They became known later as the **Scots**.
- The **Angles** were invaders from Germany who settled around Hadrian's Wall in Northumbria. They brought with them Anglo-Saxon words, which later became the Scots language.

⚙️ Activate your brain cells!

- **'Heritage'** means all the things that we have **inherited** from our ancestors that help to shape our present. Our Scottish heritage is made up of the **traditions**, **music**, **books**, **poems**, **language**, **food**, **buildings**, **famous people** and **important events** that have shaped Scotland.
- With a partner, write down the headings in bold above and list what you think makes Scotland's heritage unique for each of them.
- What does it mean to be Scottish? Explain your thoughts to a partner.
- Look at the shop below. How is this connected with our heritage?

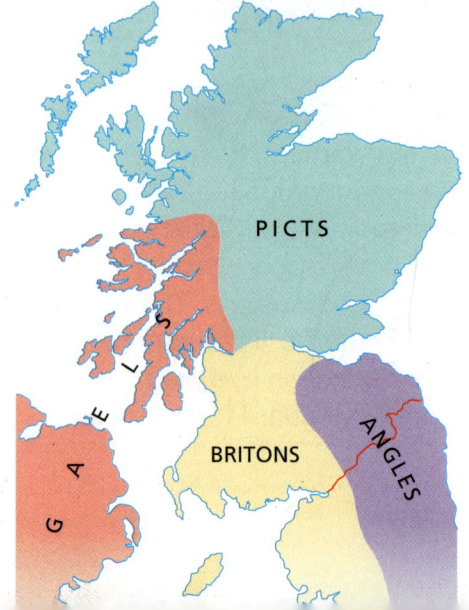

PICTS

GAELS

BRITONS

ANGLES

Kenneth MacAlpin

In AD843 the king of the Scots and Gaels of Dál Riata, Kenneth MacAlpin (*Cináed mac Ailpín*), became the leader of the Picts as well. From the 840s onwards, this new Gaelic kingdom was called **Alba** – the Gaelic name for this country. Scotland was born.

Historians debate how Kenneth MacAlpin united the three tribes.

Some historians think that many Pictish leaders were killed fighting off brutal Viking raids in AD839. While the Picts were recovering from this, Kenneth MacAlpin marched into Pictland. The Picts were no match for his huge army and surrendered. They were forced to accept MacAlpin as king in AD843.

That's a slightly outdated viewpoint. Recent investigations into this time suggest that MacAlpin may have been asked by the Picts to lead them. They needed a strong leader to help them fight off the Vikings. They were also under threat from the Angles around Hadrian's Wall. MacAlpin would have seemed like a good choice: he may even have had Pictish blood in his veins from his mother.

 ## Show your understanding

1. Make your own map of the four kingdoms. Label them with information about the different peoples.
2. Which of the following facts do you think was the most important for the birth of Scotland? Give reasons for your answer.
   - the King of the Gaels, Kenneth MacAlpin, had a huge army
   - the Picts were weakened by continuous Viking raids
   - MacAlpin's mother was a Pictish princess
   - it was not unusual for ruling families of the four kingdoms to marry each other
3. Why is your chosen fact most significant for Scotland's heritage? Turn to your partner and persuade them of its importance.
4. Choose to complete either a) or b).
   a) Write a short poem about the birth of Scotland. It doesn't have to rhyme!
   b) You work for the National Heritage organisation. Create a presentation showing the best of Scotland's heritage. Include the events of AD843, as well as your list from the beginning of this section.
   c) Using string, mark out a rough outline of Scotland on the floor. Use objects or people to show the four different tribes. Write a script and act out the story of Scotland's birth.

Explore further

Choose a kingdom to research from Picts, Britons, Gaels or Angles. Find out more about some of the following areas:
   - where did they live?
   - who led them and how were their tribes arranged?
   - what role did women play in their society?
   - religion
   - life in the tribe

What's the big deal about 1066?

What are we exploring?

By the end of this section you should be able to:

▶ Explain how a group of Vikings ended up controlling most of Britain

▶ Describe some of the ways the Normans changed Scotland

▶ Imagine the impact of the Norman invasion on Britain

How did Vikings become Normans?

The Normans were originally a tribe of Vikings. In AD911 a Norse prince called Rolf invaded northern France with his Viking army. The French king, Charles the Simple, could not defeat them and gave them a portion of France in return for peace. This became known as the Land of the North Men or Normandy. Rolf and his followers settled and built a powerful Norman nation.

What happened in 1066?

Duke William of Normandy believed he should be king of England because of a promise made to him by the old English king, Edward the Confessor. In 1066 William sailed to England and fought King Harold at Hastings. The Normans won and Harold was killed in the battle. The Bayeux Tapestry shows much of what happened.

Activate your brain cells!

What is happening in the **Bayeaux Tapestry** scene at the bottom of the page? List as many things as you can.

- Can you think of a reason why this tapestry was made?
- Imagine if cameras had not been invented. Share ideas in your class about how people could record important events around the world.

What impact did the Normans have on Scotland?

In 1071 William headed for **Alba** with his large fleet of ships and powerful army. At his capital in Dunfermline, Scotland's King Malcolm III was protecting the English prince Edgar. However, Malcolm realised he could not defend Scotland in a war against the Normans. He accepted a **truce** with the Norman king in 1072 and paid **homage** to him.

After 1100, many Norman knights were given land and power in Scotland in return for a promise to serve the Scottish king, David I. The knights acted as **sheriffs**, **judges**, **generals** and **recruiters** for David's army.

Some of the names of the Norman knights may sound familiar to you. Have you heard surnames like Stewart, de Brus (or Bruce), de Wallys (or Wallace), Bisset, Sinclair, Fraser or Grant?

The Norman knights helped to spread Norman and French literature, religion, architecture and law. French and English became the languages spoken by nobles and many townsfolk rather than Gaelic. The Normans built wooden and earth-walled castles throughout Britain. They built on naturally well-defended sites, such as rocky crags, **glacial** mounds or islands.

If no natural site could be found, they created a **motte and bailey** castle. The motte was a large man-made hill made of earth taken from a circular ditch around its base. This had a wall of wooden planks around the top. Inside was a tower, used as a lookout in peacetime and a defensive **keep** during attacks.

The **bailey** was a large flat area defended by a ditch and wooden wall. It was used for keeping animals in stables and storing food in barns. In peacetime the day-to-day living of the castle took place here.

 Show your understanding

1. Draw a storyboard showing the rise of the Normans from King Rolf to the Battle of Hastings.
2. Explain why the Scottish king David I gave Norman knights land and power.
3. Archaeological evidence of motte and bailey castles is hard to find. Why do you think this is?
4. Copy the diagram below and label it by adding the following words:

Motte / Bailey / Wood was easy to find / Built up with earth that was dug out to make a moat / Living space for the Normans / A place to which they could retreat / The moat, which gave the defenders an advantage

5. Choose to answer either **a)** or **b)**.
   a) Create a scene showing a major event in your own personal history. Try to copy the design of the Bayeaux Tapestry.
   b) Recreate one of the scenes from the Bayeaux Tapestry in your classroom, choose characters and assign roles. Take pictures and edit them on a computer to make them look like a piece of the original tapestry!

? Bore your friends...

The Bayeux Tapestry is about 20 inches high and 230 feet long. It was sewn by nuns using eight different colours of wool over a period of ten years. It contains 623 people, 202 horses, 55 dogs, 506 other birds and animals (some mythical), 49 trees, 41 ships, 37 buildings and 57 Latin inscriptions. Ask your Home Economics teacher if you can make one next term!

Migrations and invasions

23 How was society organised in Europe during the Middle Ages?

What are we exploring?

By the end of this section you should be able to:

▶ Explain what the feudal structure was

▶ Describe what life was like for peasants

▶ Imagine the world described in the Domesday Book

Activate your brain cells!

- With a partner, draw a hierarchy pyramid of your school. The person with the most power is at the top!
- Why might this be a good way to work out how other businesses are organised?

In Modern Studies, you learn about the society we live in today. It is very different from the way kings organised people in the Middle Ages. Next time you think something is unfair, spare a thought for people at the bottom of society in the Middle Ages!

People in societies throughout Europe were divided into four main groups which had different jobs to do. This way of life became known as the **feudal system**.

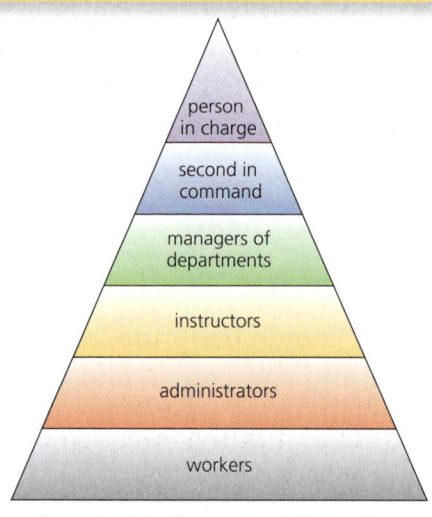

A modern business hierarchy – which system would you prefer?

Who were the peasants?

Until the nineteenth century, most people in Europe were **peasants** living in the countryside. Families worked hard in the fields and rented their land from the rich lords. People could not read or write but were very religious.

In Scotland, trees were used to make the frame of the cottages and peat or turf was used for the walls. Roofs were a framework of branches with thatched straw on top. Windows were holes in the wall with shutters to keep out the wind and rain. A fireplace in the centre of the room sat below a hole in the roof for the chimney. Animals were brought inside to sleep in a part of the house divided off by a low wall. They helped warm the cottage. The smell of the peat fire helped to soften the smell of the animals!

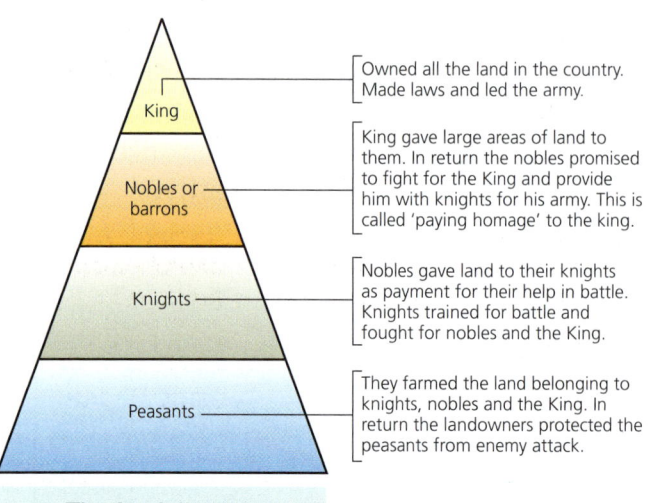

The feudal system

48

A Middle Ages house in Torthorwald, Dumfriesshire

Few peasants rode horses, most travelled on foot. There were no roads; only tracks that were muddy in winter and dusty in summer. Goods were transported to **burghs** by cattle-drawn wagons and pack horses.

What was the Domesday Book?

In 1085, William the Conqueror sent men all over England to find out about his new kingdom. They asked questions about who owned the land and what types of jobs people did. Their findings were collected in the 413-page Domesday Book.

Nothing like it had ever been made before. You can see much of it online now. It shows that in 1085 about 250 people controlled all of the land in England and only two of them were not Normans. At this time 85 per cent of the English countryside was being used for animals and crops.

What is an age?

To make understanding the past easier, historians give names to different periods or ages:

- The years before AD400 are usually called the **classical period** or ancient times.
- Between AD400 and AD1450, European peoples lived in the feudal system. This time is known as the **Middle Ages** or sometimes the **medieval** period.
- After AD1450 there were important new discoveries in sciences like chemistry, physics and astronomy. European explorers sailed long distances to find out more about the world. This is sometimes called the **Early Modern Age** and was the beginning of the **Modern Age**, which we still live in today.

 Show your understanding

1. Answer the following questions about feudal society:
   - who is the richest person and which group is the poorest?
   - which group has to provide food for knights?
   - which group gets land from barons?
2. Why is a survey such as the Domesday Book useful for a king? What was its purpose? What facts did it record?
3. Make a Domesday Book for the class! Apart from names and ages, what facts about your class could you record? Make your book look old and authentic.

Name of landowner: deMontford	Number of peasants on land: 36	Number of slaves on property: 1	Number of female slaves on property: 2	Number of priests on property: 1	Number of churches on property: 1
Ploughs: 24	Fishponds: 3	Cattle: 49	Cows: 26	Pigs: 15	Sheep: 23
Amount of meadow land: 26 acres	Amount of woodland: 32 acres	Number of watermills: 0 acres	Wild horses: 0 acres	Beehives: 2 acres	Goats: 0 acres

24 How did the burghs grow?

What are we exploring?

By the end of this section you should be able to:

▶ Explain how Scotland's burghs began

▶ Describe where and what people traded

▶ Imagine what life was like in a medieval burgh

 Activate your brain cells!

- How would you describe the **centre** of your city, town or village? What goes on there?
- In pairs, write down the names of as many shops as you can that are located on your high street. Make a list of what they sell or provide next to the shop name.
- Why have these shops chosen to open on the high street?

The Merket Cross in Haddington. Is there a market cross where you live? Why is it still there?

The first real towns were not built in Scotland until around 1150. They were known as **burghs** and began as **trading centres**. By 1500 there were about 150 burghs in Scotland. Most were the size of modern villages, with between 500 and 1000 **inhabitants**.

Each burgh had a market place where people could buy fresh produce from the surrounding countryside. Travellers wanting to come into the burgh had to pay **tolls** (taxes) before they were allowed in. Some **Royal Burghs** were given special privileges by the king to trade overseas.

Ships from Germany, the Netherlands and France sailed into the harbours of Dundee, Aberdeen and Leith. These coastal towns were in the right place to take advantage of the increase in European trade in the 12th and 13th centuries.

As the towns grew, some Scots became rich. This led to a growing demand for luxury goods such as wine, fabrics and food from overseas. Many foreign traders lived in Scotland and brought new cultural ideas and architectural styles with them.

What were Scotland's first towns like?

Wealthy merchants called **burgesses** controlled the trade of the burgh. They joined together to create a burgh council and collected taxes on the goods that were traded. They also arranged for the streets to be swept and thieves to be punished.

Several craftspeople worked in the burgh: cloth-makers, bakers, leatherworkers, blacksmiths, tailors, jewellers, weavers, candle-makers, shoe-makers, butchers, bakers, fishmongers, builders and carpenters. Many had a sign above their doors with a symbol on it to tell people what their craft was.

The streets were dusty in summer and muddy in winter. Rubbish and toilet waste were often thrown out of the window! Middens piled up on every street. People rarely bathed and disease spread because of bad health and poor sanitation.

As towns grew, poor landless people moved there looking for work. Some became servants or labourers; lucky ones trained for a skilled career. Many were homeless and had to beg to survive.

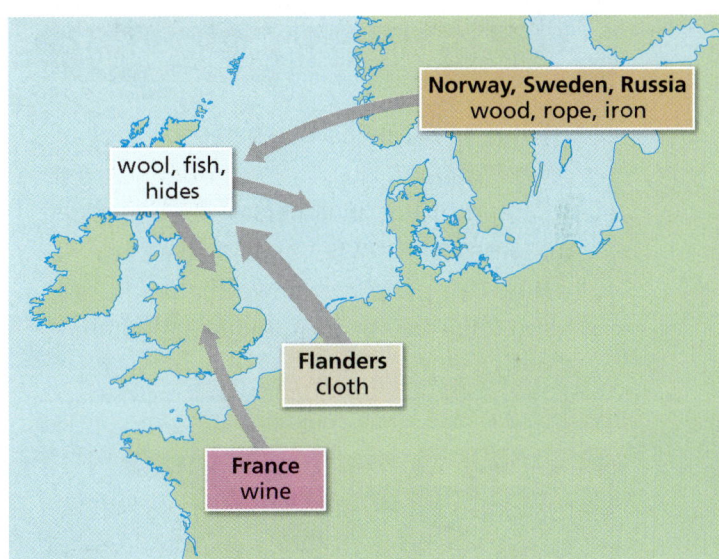

Norway, Sweden, Russia
wood, rope, iron

wool, fish, hides

Flanders
cloth

France
wine

Show your understanding

1. Write a sentence or two explaining what went on in the burgh. Include the following words:

   burgh   trade   market cross   buy

2. Why do you think most Royal Burghs were on the east coast of Scotland?

3. Copy the sentences below and finish them with the correct words.
   - Most of the trade to and from Scotland was carried by sea / land / river.
   - Goods that are sent out from a country are called exports / imports.

4. Choose to answer either **a)** or **b)**.
   a) Copy and complete the following table using the map.

Goods that were exported from Scotland	Goods that were imported into Scotland

   b) According to the size of the arrows on the map, which countries did Scottish merchants trade the most with? Why do you think this was?

5. Draw a suitable sign for each of the following: ale-maker, butcher and goldsmith. Now draw one for your chosen medieval profession.

Collect a skill

Comparing life then and now

In pairs, look at the picture of a medieval burgh. Describe as many features of life there as you can. Then turn to a pair near you and share ideas.

1 How many things are different to the way we live now? How many are similar?

2 Imagine you are in the scene. What noises do you hear? Record some sounds using a microphone.

3 If you could go back in time to the medieval burgh, which of the jobs listed in the text would you do? Why?

25 What was so 'Magna' about the Great Charter of 1215?

What are we exploring?

By the end of this section you should be able to:

▶ Explain what promises were made in the Magna Carta
▶ Describe why it is such an important document
▶ Understand how relationships between kings and their people have changed over time

 Activate your brain cells!

- What can it mean if a person is 'out of control'?
- Can you think of a person for whom there are no rules to control them?
- How can people in power be made to use their power for good rather than bad?

The **Magna Carta** is one of the most important documents in European history. It was an agreement between King John of England and his **nobles**. It took some power away from harsh kings and gave the people some rights.

John ruled from AD1199 to AD1216 and was a strong king with a fierce temper. He kept his nobles under tight control. In 1215 they **rebelled** and he faced losing his crown. He was forced to sign the Magna Carta by the Thames, at Runnymede.

The agreement contained 63 promises. Some of them are about rights that every person in a free country should have today – including you. After 1215, when there was any trouble about how kings used their power, people went back to the Magna Carta.

The Magna Carta memorial at Runnymede

Read some of the promises below.

I, King John of England, promise to my archbishops, bishops, barons, officials and all loyal subjects that…

Promises to lords and knights

Barons should pay me no more than 100 pounds for using my land. Knights should pay five pounds. I must not ask for extra payments from lords and knights unless they agree to pay more.

> **? Bore your friends...**
>
> *Magna Carta is Latin for Great Charter. A charter is an agreement or contract.*

Promises about law and justice

I will not deny anyone a fair trial. No free man shall be seized or imprisoned. No man shall be stripped of his rights or possessions. No man shall be outlawed or exiled unless a proper trial finds him guilty.

A promise about keeping his promises

The barons shall elect 25 of their number to keep the peace and freedoms promised in this document. This council will become known as the 'Lords'. If I want to make any decisions that change freedom in the country, I must ask these lords first. I swear that these promises shall be kept in good faith and without cheating.

The birth of parliament

In 1275, Edward I needed to raise taxes for his wars. He asked the knights and townsmen, the '**Commons**', to join the **Lords** in the council. Their meeting was called **parliament**.

From then on, when the king wanted an important law passed he asked the Lords and the Commons to agree to it. When they agreed it was called an **Act of Parliament**. Over the next century other countries in Europe followed with their own parliaments, including Scotland.

This building was built in 1834, but parliament began at Runnymede in 1215

Show your understanding

1. Write a sentence or two to explain why the Magna Carta has been described as one of the most important primary sources in Britain's history.
2. Read your partner's answer to question 1. How could you improve their answer?
3. Why do you think the Magna Carta memorial at Runnymede was built? What other memorials can you name?
4. Today, no one accused of a crime can be left in prison without a fair trial. Which one of the Magna Carta promises made sure of this?
5. Which people in the feudal society were left out of Edward I's parliament?
6. Which two sections of parliament today are the same as Edwards I's first parliament?
7. Why might the Magna Carta be an important historical document for students of Modern Studies?
8. Make your own Magna Carta. Use the promises and the words at the beginning and end. Make a seal in card or wax to go on it. How could you make this document look old?

How would you attack a castle?

What are we exploring?

By the end of this section you should be able to:

▶ Explain how castles became stronger

▶ Describe methods of attack and defence

▶ Visit and research your nearest castle

 Activate your brain cells!

- How did builders improve the design of a castle? Write down as many ideas as you can with your partner.
- Be the expert – volunteer to tell the class about changing castles.

To stay at the top of the feudal system, a knight, baron or king needed a good castle to control his land and people.

As buildings improved, **motte and bailey** castles were replaced by **stone** castles. These were much more difficult to attack because it was impossible to set fire to them. The remains of stone castles can be seen in most parts of Scotland. The baileys were still used, but a stone keep was built on top and a stone wall surrounded it. By the 13th century, castles became more sophisticated. Examples can be seen at Dirleton in East Lothian and Bothwell in Lanarkshire.

How to attack a castle!

Siege

Attackers would simply surround the castle and wait. They would try to starve the defenders into submission.

Bothwell Castle

Battering ram

Used to ram a wooden log against the castle door or wall to make a hole in the defences and get into the castle. How easy do you think this method was?

Siege tower

Built of wood, the siege tower was rolled on its wheels to the castle wall and attackers could walk up it to clamber over the top.

Catapult

Used to throw large boulders at the castle walls in an attempt to knock them down. This catapult was effective but was tricky to reload and needed to be built on site. The Romans first used these and they were used throughout the Middle Ages.

Mining

Attackers would dig under the castle walls, holding their tunnel up with wooden stakes. These stakes would then be set on fire, the tunnels would collapse and the walls above them would fall to the ground!

Bribery

Attackers could secretly bribe inhabitants of the castle to let them in. Once inside, they could open the gates and let their armies in.

How to defend a castle

It was important to build your castle so that it could be easily **defended** against any enemies. There were many ways to do this:

- Build walls that were high and up to 2.4 metres thick.
- Protect the main entrance with a **portcullis** and **drawbridge**. The portcullis could be dropped and the drawbridge raised at times of attack.
- Surround your castle with a wide, deep ditch filled with water called a **moat**.
- Build **battlements** along the top walls and protect archers as they fire on the enemy.
- Build **arrow slits** into walls so that the archers could shoot arrows from inside the castle.
- Build **machicolation** holes in the walls that allowed hot oil or sand to be poured onto the enemy. This seeped inside their armour and burned them!

Show your understanding

1. Would you rather attack or defend a castle? Why?
2. Choose to answer a) or b).
   a) Make a set of attack and defence Top Trumps cards like this one.

Method: Laying siege		**ATTACK**
(Image)		Description
Cost	_____	out of 5
Speed	_____	of 5
Easy	_____	of 5
Danger to own men	_____	of 5
Overall effectiveness	_____	out of 20

   b) Imagine you are a medieval king attacking Dunbar Castle. Write a battle diary to explain why you chose your method of attack.

Explore further

Investigate a local castle and produce a project about it. Answer questions such as: When was it built? What was it like to live there? Why was it built? What battles did it play a part in? Who built it? What is it like now? Your finished project must have all of the following **success criteria**:

- detailed written information
- accurate historical facts and a map
- pictures and/or photographs of the castle as it was then and is now
- colourful and imaginative design

27 What did Europeans believe in before the spread of Christianity?

What are we exploring?

By the end of this section you should be able to:

▶ Explain the difference between Pagan and Christian religions

▶ Describe some Pagan beliefs

▶ Imagine how Christianity spread alongside these beliefs before becoming the main religion in Europe

A **Pagan** believes in many different gods or spirits. European people worshipped in this way from the Stone Age and continued to do so for a long time after the birth of Christ.

The religion that celebrates the life of Christ, Christianity, worships just one god. It took hundreds of years for Christianity to become the main religion of Europe. It was not a quick **conversion**.

Strange beliefs?

Until the ninth century AD, most Celtic and Barbarian tribes in Europe were Pagans. They worshipped the Sun, the Moon and the seasons and they also believed in mythical gods and spirits.

We know very little about Pagan beliefs. Historians have begun to piece them together by investigating ancient idols, carvings and stones. Each tribe seems to have had its own special Earth goddess who helped the crops grow well. Some tribes gave animal **sacrifices** to gods in the hope of a good harvest or to avoid problems. Sometimes even people were sacrificed.

Activate your brain cells!

- In a group, list the ways in which you could survive a parachute jump if the parachute didn't open!
- Most challenges in life don't have one solution or answer. What solutions does religion give people?

Tombs and stones

Before Christianity, the tombs of important tribal families were designed like houses. How do we remember and honour our ancestors today?

Britain has many ancient stone circles and standing stones. Most were put up centuries before the birth of Christ. They may have been used to worship the Sun or the stars or to map out the seasons and plan when to plant and harvest crops.

The stones were cut and shaped using simple tools and were transported using only ropes and logs.

Callanish stone circle, Lewis

Druids and celebrations

Druids were important religious people among the Celts of Europe from as early as 1500BC. Druids acted as judges, doctors and mystical teachers. They were respected as the wisest members of their societies.

Celtic tribes celebrated **Bealltainn** at the beginning of the summer season, when herds of livestock could be put out to pasture on the new grassland. Later on, they marked the end of the harvest period at the end of October with the festival of **Samhuinn**.

The Gaels believed that Samhuinn was a time when the distance between this world and the underworld became narrowest. They lit bonfires and young men wore masks, pretended to be dead and carried lanterns made from hollowed-out turnips.

The annual Beltane festival on Edinburgh's Calton Hill

Mixing religions

As Christianity spread, the ideas of the Christians and Celtic Pagan tribes mixed together. This can be seen clearly on this stone from Glamis in Angus. It is probably the oldest stone to show a cross. Can you also see some Pictish symbols?

Show your understanding

1. Write a sentence or two to explain a simple difference between Pagan beliefs and Christianity.
2. The Romans described the religious practices of northern Britain as cannibalistic. What evidence can you find to back this up?
3. How and when are the ideas of Samhuinn still practised today?
4. Choose to answer either a) or b).
   a) **Team challenge!**
   Your team has to move a slab of stone 20 miles across rough and boggy ground. Plan how you are going to do this. What roles will your team have? Draw a diagram or make a model of your solution.
   b) **Facthenge!**
   Make a model of Stonehenge out of boxes. Cover it in paper, and write as many facts about Pagan beliefs as you can find on it. Your aim is to cover the whole of Stonehenge in quality information!

Explore further

Ask your RME teacher for information about Paganism and about where Pagans exist today.

How did Christianity change Britain?

What are we exploring?

By the end of this section you should be able to:

▶ Explain how Christianity spread through Europe

▶ Tell someone about the lives of St Ninian and St Columba

▶ Imagine how important the church was to medieval people

How did Christianity spread?

In the Middle Ages Christianity replaced Pagan beliefs to play a central role in people's lives.

In AD 306 Constantine became the first Christian Emperor of Rome. Over the next century the church sent monks into Europe as **missionaries** to teach Christianity. In time, Celts and Barbarians became Christians and churches and monasteries were built all over Europe.

The first man to teach the ideas of Christianity in Scotland was St Ninian. In AD397 he was made a bishop in Rome and set off to Scotland as the first Scottish missionary. He set up a church in Whithorn in southern Scotland at around the time the Romans left for good.

Activate your brain cells!

- If you could be just one of the following, would you choose to be:
  - famous
  - wise
  - beautiful
  - rich
  - happy
  - healthy?
- Discuss how you can plan for these things.
- Imagine you were a peasant in the Middle Ages. Which one would you choose?

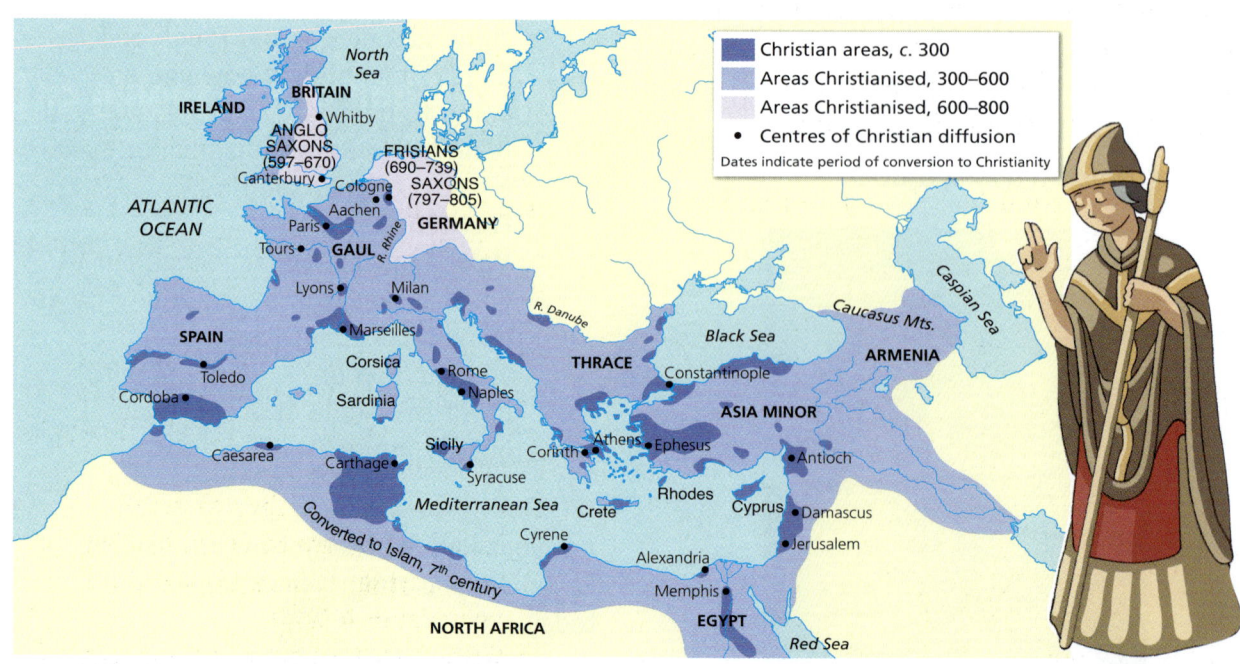

Christian areas, c. 300
Areas Christianised, 300–600
Areas Christianised, 600–800
• Centres of Christian diffusion
Dates indicate period of conversion to Christianity

North Sea
BRITAIN
IRELAND
Whitby
ANGLO SAXONS (597–670)
Canterbury
Cologne
FRISIANS (690–739)
SAXONS (797–805)
Aachen
GERMANY
ATLANTIC OCEAN
Paris
GAUL
R. Rhine
Tours
Lyons
Milan
R. Danube
Caucasus Mts.
Caspian Sea
SPAIN
Marseilles
Black Sea
ARMENIA
Toledo
Corsica
Rome
THRACE
Constantinople
Cordoba
Sardinia
Naples
ASIA MINOR
Caesarea
Carthage
Sicily
Syracuse
Corinth
Athens
Ephesus
Antioch
Rhodes
Cyprus
Damascus
Mediterranean Sea
Crete
Jerusalem
Cyrene
Alexandria
Converted to Islam, 7th century
Memphis
NORTH AFRICA
EGYPT
Red Sea

Holy men were made saints when they died if they did good things for Christianity. Other missionaries followed Ninian. Their job of converting the Pagan Picts was not easy. Most people could not read or write, but the monks kept holy books and made beautiful copies of them.

St Columba

Colum Cille built the monastery at **Iona** in AD563. During Columba's time Iona was a busy centre for travellers and missionaries from Ireland and all over the world.

We know about Columba from a book written 100 years after his death by an Abbott at Iona called Adamnan. Among other stories, the book tells us that Columba had visions of the future, won a magic contest against the King of the Picts and calmed a mysterious creature on the shores of Loch Ness.

When he died, Columba's bones (**relics**) were stored in a box called the **Monymusk Reliquary**. It became the holiest object in medieval Scotland.

The power of the church

Over the next few centuries, the church became the most powerful thing in most people's lives. It could fine, whip or put peasants in the stocks for getting drunk, not going to church, gambling, swearing or even shaving their beard on a Sunday!

Land and money

Everyone had to pay a tax called a **tithe**. Farmers had to give the church one tenth of their newborn livestock and crops each year. Some had to pay rent because the church owned their land and house. This made the church very rich and powerful.

The church gave people help

Medieval life was hard with the threats of starvation and disease and poor education. The church helped in simple ways. For example the churchyard was used for events like weddings, feasts and dances to cheer people up.

Priests, monks and nuns believed it was their duty to help the sick and grew herbs and plants to make medicines. The church encouraged rich people to give **alms** (share their money). Some built alms houses for old people to live in.

Show your understanding

1. Do research and write a fact file on St Ninian or St Columba, include pictures.
2. Is Adamnan's book about Columba a primary or secondary source? Why? What problems might a historian have with his book?
3. Draw a table to compare the ways in which the church controlled people's lives and ways in which it helped people in the Middle Ages.
4. Choose to answer **either** a) or b).
   a) Imagine you are St Columba. Get your partner to interview you for the position of a saint.
   b) Write a CV for Columba's application for the job of saint!

29 How did the Muslim faith grow?

What are we exploring?

By the end of this section you should be able to:

▶ Explain some of the main beliefs of Islam
▶ Describe how the Muslim faith grew bigger in the Middle Ages
▶ Identify some ways in which Islam changed Europe and the Middle East

Activate your brain cells!

- How many different religions can you name?
- Ask your partner what they know about Muslim people and their faith.
- Which of these people are Muslim? (Answer at the bottom of the page).

In AD610, a man called Mohammed started to teach a new religion in Arabia. This religion became known as **Islam** and its followers were called **Muslims**.

The history of Islam is fascinating and changed the world forever. It has never been more important for us to understand the Muslim faith. Extreme groups carrying out terrorist acts have damaged the image of Islam in the 21st century. There are many different ideas about what it means to be a Muslim.

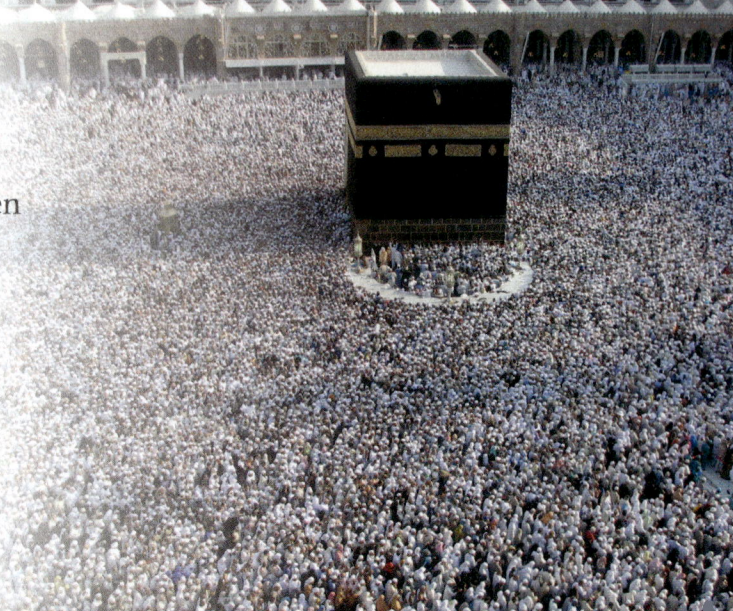

Answer: All of them! Does that surprise you?

Mohammed's message

Ask your RME teacher about Islam. Here are some key ideas to kickstart your learning…

- People should obey **Allah** – the one true God.
- Muslims should pray five times a day.
- **Mosques** should be built for prayer.
- A Muslim priest is called an **Imam**.
- Muslims should give money to the poor of society.
- Muslims should go without food and drink during daylight hours in the month called **Ramadan**.
- Men have the right to choose their own wives and can have more than one.
- All Muslims should try to go on a pilgrimage to **Mecca** – the holy city of Islam.
- Mohammed claims to have been visited by Allah, and Islam's holy book, the **Koran**, contains messages from Allah to Mohammed.

How did Islam spread?

Mohammed began preaching in Mecca but the rich city merchants forced him out in AD622. He escaped to a town called Medina. Two years later his group was attacked by an army from Mecca. Mohammed fought bravely and defeated his people's enemies at the Battle of al Badr. After his victory, many people supported Mohammed and became Muslims.

Mohammed died in AD632 and the Muslims were ruled by a series of leaders called the **Caliphs**. They fought many battles to gain land for their people and to spread the Muslim religion. The Caliphs were rich and lived in luxury palaces in Baghdad (the capital of modern-day Iraq).

In AD661 Islam was split into two groups, who argued over who should be the next Caliph. Today the **Sunni** version of Islam is practised in Saudi Arabia while the competing **Shi'a** version remains in Iran. They still argue over which group has the right to lead Muslims.

By AD750 the two groups had built a vast Islamic Empire, stretching from northern India to Spain. This empire included **Jerusalem** – a holy place to both Jews and Christians.

The Muslim religion was also spread by trade. Arab traders made journeys throughout the Islamic Empire and beyond. They took their religion with them and sometimes settled in far-off places.

Show your understanding

1. Explain briefly why the message of Mohammed appealed to some people.
2. Here are six sentences – some are true and some are false. Correct the false ones by rewriting the statements.
   - Muslims are easy to identify.
   - Muslims should pray three times a day.
   - The holy city of Islam is Jerusalem.
   - The holy book of Islam is the Koran.
   - Islam has been divided into the Sunni and Shi'a groups for a brief time.
   - The Islamic Empire was huge.
3. Put these dates in the right order. Beside each date, write what happened in that year.
   AD622 AD750 AD610 AD632 AD661 AD624
4. Describe two ways in which Islam spread.

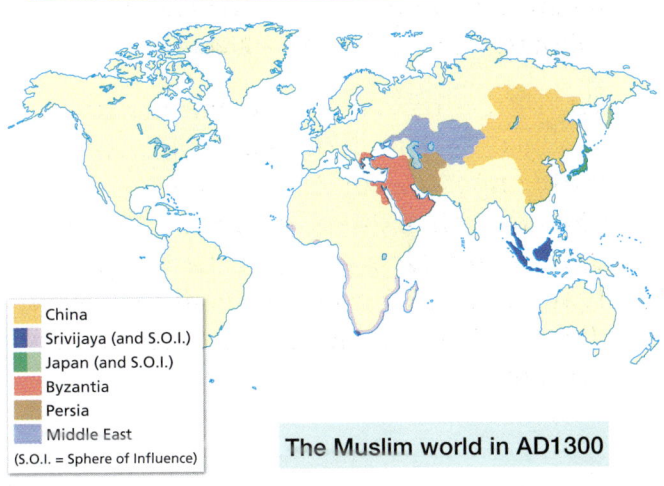

	China
	Srivijaya (and S.O.I.)
	Japan (and S.O.I.)
	Byzantia
	Persia
	Middle East
(S.O.I. = Sphere of Influence)

The Muslim world in AD1300

What happens when two religions clash?

What are we exploring?

What are we exploring?
By the end of this section you should be able to:

▶ Explain what the Crusades were

▶ Describe what happened in each Crusade

▶ Imagine how relations between Muslims and Christians were affected by the Crusades

A **holy war** is a war fought over religion. Some historians argue that religion has started more wars in the past than any other factor. Others argue that leaders have often used religion as an excuse to start wars to get land or power. Some of the most **infamous** and bloody holy wars happened when Christianity clashed with Islam.

In 1060 **Palestine** was controlled by Muslims from Turkey. Palestine was the Holy Land for Christians and Jews. The Turks threatened Christian visitors to Palestine and

 Activate your brain cells!

- Ask your partner one of these questions and listen to their answer without interrupting:
  - What do you think about money?
  - What do you think about boys/girls?
- Swap over and give them your opinion.
- Did you disagree on anything? Why do people sometimes have different opinions?

The Holy Land of Palestine in 1060

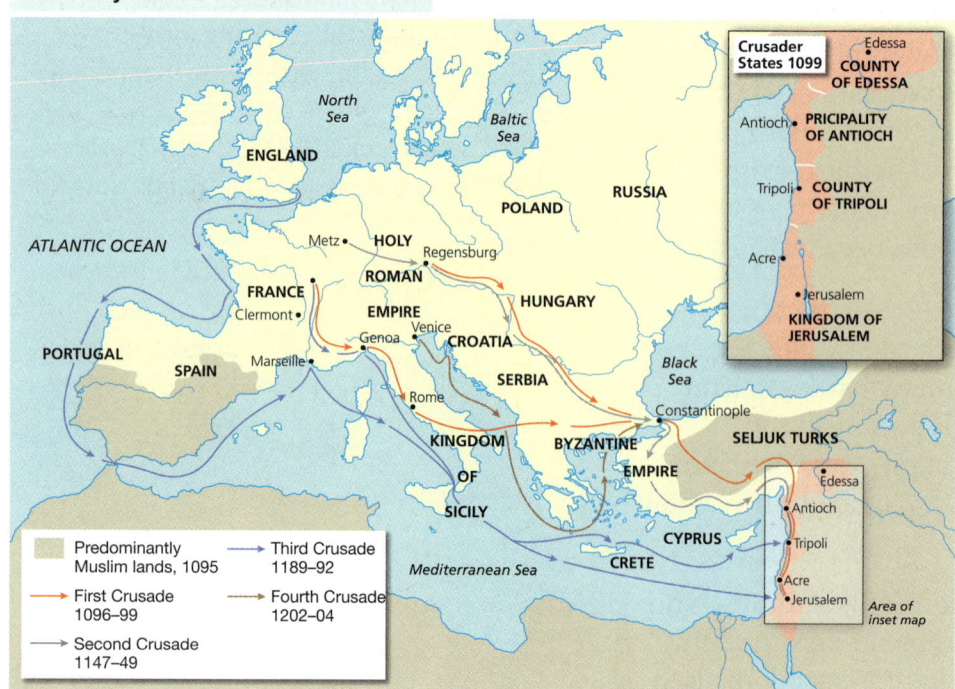

Crusader States 1099
COUNTY OF EDESSA
PRICIPALITY OF ANTIOCH
COUNTY OF TRIPOLI
KINGDOM OF JERUSALEM

Predominantly Muslim lands, 1095

First Crusade 1096–99

Second Crusade 1147–49

Third Crusade 1189–92

Fourth Crusade 1202–04

VRBANVS II. Gallus, creatus die
12. Martij an. 1088, Sedit an. ii. mens. 4.
dies 18. Obijt die 29. Iulij ann. 1099.
Vac. Sed. dies 14.

attacked Christian lands. Christians felt their religion was in danger and asked the **Pope** for help.

In 1095 Pope Urban II saw a way to get all the Christian peoples of Europe to support him and so increase his own power. He urged Christians from all over Europe to fight a holy war to drive out the Muslims from the Holy Land. It became known as the **Crusade**.

The People's Crusade

The Pope's messengers spread false stories about terrible atrocities committed by the Turks against Christians. Large crowds set out to walk to the Holy Land and save Palestine from the Turks, whom they called the **infidels** or non-believers. The mass movement of these groups became known as the '**People's Crusade**'.

The groups wandered through Europe causing more harm than good. Some slaughtered Jews and Pagans in Hungary and Germany and were killed as a result. Only two groups reached Constantinople, only to be killed by the Turkish troops.

The 'real' First Crusade, 1096–1099

Christian nobles and kings gathered armies from among their people in France, Germany and Italy. Highly skilled knights who were also monks joined these armies. The most famous groups of warrior-monks were the **Knights Templar**, the **Teutonic Knights** from Germany and the **Knights Hospitaler**.

In 1099 they captured Jerusalem. Their siege of the city has been described by eyewitnesses as a strange mixture of religion and killing. Accounts from the Crusaders themselves leave little doubt that there was great slaughter after the siege.

The Crusaders set up a new kingdom they called the '**Outremer**' or 'The Kingdom across the Mediterranean Sea'. They left the Outremer weak by returning home in large numbers. The Muslim forces struck back and seized the town of Edessa.

30 What happens when two religions clash? (*cont.*)

The siege of Jerusalem

Second Crusade, 1147–1149

This Crusade was a failed attempt to recapture Edessa from the Muslims. Under their leader **Saladin**, the Muslims recaptured Jerusalem.

Third Crusade, 1189–1192

This Crusade was led by **King Richard 'The Lion Heart'** of England and the rulers of France and Germany. The Crusaders won many battles and recaptured the city of Acre, but did not recapture Jerusalem.

Fourth crusade, 1202–1204

This Crusade only got as far as Constantinople. Although the Crusaders were on the same side as the people of Constantinople, they decided to **raid** it and **steal** many of its treasures.

How did the Crusades end?

In 1229 the Muslims agreed that the Christians could have Jerusalem back, but this agreement did not last. The Muslims continued to win back land and in 1291 they conquered Acre, the last remaining Crusader city. The Crusades had ended in failure.

Show your understanding

1. Write a sentence or two explaining who fought who in the Crusades.
2. Why did Pope Urban II order the Crusades? Explain your thoughts to a partner and then to the rest of the class.
3. What effect do you think the Crusades have had on the relationship between Muslims and Christians?
4. Answer either a) or b)
   a) Storyboard the siege of Jerusalem in 1099. Use the images here for ideas, as well as your work on attacking a castle.
   b) Write a poem to tell future students about the Crusades. It doesn't have to rhyme!

Source A – from a Turkish eyewitness to the recapture of Jerusalem

Our great leader Saladin is a most generous and gracious man. He fought bravely against the murdering Christians and won back Jerusalem for us. He showed the Templar Knights mercy where they had shown us and the good people of Jerusalem none. When we forced the knights out of the city, the people came to us and thanked us for saving them. I don't know how the Christian god allows his holy knights to steal, drink and murder without punishment. It is not a god I'd wish to serve. All praise Allah!

Source B – from a report on the battle sent by the Pope's messenger

Saladin showed no mercy to our knights or the people of Jerusalem. The infidel had his men slaughter all in their way. Our men fought bravely and with God on their side. But they were outnumbered by a swarm of murderous Muslims. Their god is an evil being. The people of Jerusalem are now crying with fear.

Collect a skill

Understanding bias

This skill is all about being able to spot different opinions and preferences. Writers might have preferred one person, place or religion to another. As a result, what they write might not be the truth. Sources can often be affected by **bias**. Look at the two primary sources about the Second Crusade.

1. Copy and complete the following table.

	Source A	Source B
Words used to describe Saladin		
Words used to describe the Crusaders		

2. Why might these two sources have different opinions?
3. Which source do you think is right about Saladin and the Crusaders? Can you explain why?
4. Write a script for a debate between two people over an issue. It could be about whether cheese is tasty or horrible, if aliens exist or not... anything you like! One person should argue for something and the other against. Act out this script with a partner.

31 How did a flea bite plunge Europe into crisis?

By the end of this section you should be able to:

▶ Explain what the plague was

▶ Describe the effects of the plague on people and society

▶ Imagine how the plague changed Europe forever

The **plague** was the first ever mass **epidemic** and changed the world forever. It killed millions of Europeans.

Rats lived in the filthy conditions of medieval towns and villages. Fleas lived on the fur of the rats, and when they fed on the rats' blood they became infected with the **bubonic plague bacteria**. When humans were bitten by the fleas the plague bacteria entered their bloodstream.

Activate your brain cells!

- Can you think of any recent outbreaks of disease? Explain to a partner any ways in which they have changed how you live or think.
- What would happen if a disease killed one in four of the people in the room? Act it out to see who gets the disease!

How did it start?

In 1347 a trading ship returned to Italy from Asia. Rats on board spread the plague, killing one in four people in Europe over the next 100 years – about 400 million people! People believed the plague was God's punishment for their sins.

Signs of the plague

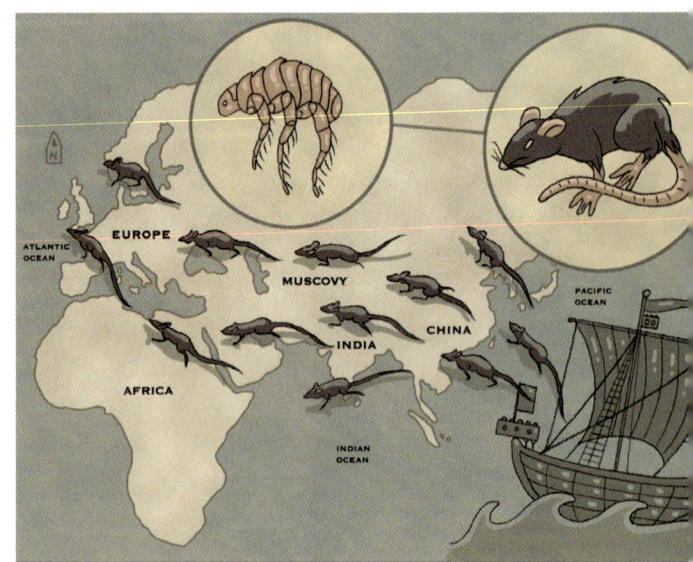

Source A – Leuan Gethin (a Welsh Poet) in 1349

We see death coming amongst us like black smoke. Woe is the shilling in the armpit; it is a terrible, painful and angry boil. A harmful thing of black colour… an ugly eruption which comes with terrible haste.

Source B – a Scottish Survivor of the plague

The plague attacks the common people but rarely the rich. It is a strange and fearful kind of death. First come the evil boils, black on the body or the face. Your flesh swells and puffs up around the infection and you drag out the rest of your earthly life in agony. Mercifully you will die just two days after the first **buboe** appears.

The **buboes** were a sign of the fatal disease but doctors did not really know how to explain where the plague came from or the fact that it developed in dirty conditions.

Strange ideas to cure the plague included…

- Bleed the patient of all the bad blood in his or her body.
- Give strong medicine to cause diarrhoea or vomiting to get rid of bad fluids.
- Burn the local witches whose evil spells have brought plague to the land.
- Find any Jewish man in the village for they are bound to be responsible.
- Put a live frog on the plague boil. The frog will swell up and burst. Keep doing this until the frogs stop bursting.

 Show your understanding

1. Draw a diagram showing how the plague was spread.
2. According to Source B, the plague attacked peasants but rarely the richer people in society. Why do you think the poor were hardest hit?
3. What evidence is there that people in the Middle Ages did not understand how the human body works or how disease spread?
4. Use this list and a map of Europe to record the spread of the plague:
   - October 1347: reported in Sicily from a ship from Asia
   - March 1348: rest of Italy
   - April: Spain
   - June: Paris
   - August: first reports in England
   - November: London
   - January 1349: Scotland, Wales and Ireland.
5. Describe what the plague did to people. Draw gruesome pictures to match your writing!

How did the plague affect Europe?

Famine

Millions of the peasants killed had been relied upon to farm and produce crops for people to eat in the villages and cities. Many people living in towns died of starvation.

Uprising

English peasants revolted in 1381 against the taxes they had to give to kings and landlords during such an unhappy time. More peasants moved from the country to the towns.

Benefits

Death led to a shortage of workers. The peasants were able to demand more money and better conditions from landowners by the sixteenth century. This destroyed the feudal system forever.

What happens when the line of kings is broken?

What are we exploring?

By the end of this section you should be able to:

▶ Explain how Alexander III's death led to a crisis in Scotland

▶ Describe the role played by Edward I in the crisis

▶ Connect the death of Alexander III with the Scottish Wars of Independence

This is the story of the death of Alexander III. Scots look back on his death as a great tragedy. The Scottish line of kings was broken and Scotland was thrown into **crisis**. The shortage of anyone to replace him led to terrible wars with England that lasted for more than 100 years.

 Activate your brain cells!

- If you could choose anyone to become king or queen of Britain, who would you choose? Don't just choose yourself!
- Why might people disagree with you? Does the rest of the class agree with you? Can you think of a way to make everyone happy?

What happened?

On 18 March 1286, King Alexander III held a meeting of his **Grand Council** in Edinburgh Castle. Outside, a violent storm raged. When the meeting was over, the king was determined to travel to Kinghorn in Fife, where his beloved Queen Yolande was staying. The king's advisers pleaded with him not to travel but Alexander ignored them and left to cross at the queen's ferry.

Despite the weather, Alexander reached the other side safely and set off on horseback along the narrow path by the seashore, but he became separated from his guides. The next morning he was found lying at the bottom of a cliff with a broken neck. In the darkness his horse probably stumbled and fell, throwing Alexander to his death. The spot is now marked with this **memorial**.

Alexander's nearest heir was his granddaughter Margaret, the Maid of Norway. She was three years old and could not run the country. King Edward I of England thought this was a perfect chance to join England and Scotland together and arranged that Margaret should marry his son.

The Scots nobles argued about letting this marriage take place. They demanded that if England and Scotland ever had one ruler, all the rights and laws of Scotland should be protected. In 1290, the seven-year-old Margaret sailed from Norway. She became ill on the journey and died in the Orkney Islands. Scotland had to find a new ruler.

How was this problem solved?

I am descended from ancient Scottish kings. I claim that I am the rightful heir to the throne. I should be king!

Show your understanding

1. Why was Alexander's death a problem for Scotland?
2. Why did Bishop Fraser ask King Edward to come to the border?
3. Was Bishop Fraser right?
4. What do you think were Edward I's motives for getting involved in the crisis?
5. Choose to answer a), b) or c).

   a) Create a storyboard of the events from the meeting in Edinburgh to Edward I's decision.

   b) Write a script for a play called *Death of a King*. List all the characters involved and write out their lines.

   c) Make up a song or a rap about the death of Alexander. Stick to the facts but let your creative ideas flow!

*I will decide who will be the next king of Scotland. In return the men who want to be king must accept me as their **overlord**. The two best **claimants** are John Balliol and Robert Bruce. After thinking things over, I declare that John Balliol has the best right to the throne.*

King Edward I of England

The lords and bishops of Scotland will accept Edward's decision. We need a king. There is great fear of a general war and a great slaughter of men if the thirteen argue amongst themselves. Let King Edward come with troops to the border, to help save the shedding of blood, and choose the next king of Scotland.

Bishop Fraser of St Andrews

Collect a skill

Family trees

Understanding how a family tree diagram works is a very useful skill.

1. Study the family tree of Alexander III.
   a) What does the symbol '=' mean?
   b) What does 'd. *date*' mean?
   c) Who was the grandson of William I?
   d) What relation were William I and David, Earl of Huntingdon?
   e) Weighing up all the evidence, who do you think should have been king of Scotland?

2. Draw your own family tree. How far up the tree can you go?

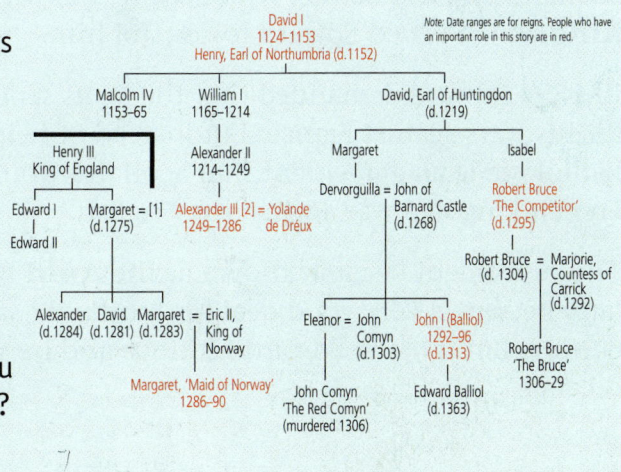

What did the Hammer do to the Puppet?

What are we exploring?

By the end of this section you should be able to:
- Explain how Edward I and John Balliol got their nicknames
- Describe how Edward I took control of Scotland
- Imagine how Scots felt towards Edward I

 Activate your brain cells!

- What are your top five favourite possessions?
- Are they part of what makes who you are?
- How would you feel if they were taken away from you?
- Why might kings take things away from countries under their control?

King Edward I's control of Scotland became increasingly violent. His aim to drive Scottish rebels into the ground like a nail into wood earned him the nickname the **Hammer of the Scots**.

The new king

King John Balliol was crowned at Scone on St Andrew's Day in 1292. Edward I made it clear that he was the real ruler of Scotland and not Balliol, who became known as a **puppet king** who allowed Edward to control him.

In 1294 Edward demanded that the Scots send him troops for his wars against France. But instead of helping Edward, Balliol made an agreement that Scotland would help the French king in a war against the English.

This agreement became known as the **Auld Alliance**. It later became a very good deal for Scotland's safety and culture. But it made Edward I furious and he sought revenge.

Source A

The Hammer strikes a terrible blow

Edward led his army to Berwick in 1296. He ordered his troops to viciously butcher the townsfolk.

Balliol's troops rode out to meet the English army but were virtually destroyed at the battle of Dunbar. Edward continued to march north, destroying the countryside and capturing many castles. Meanwhile, most Scots nobles rushed to tell him how loyal they were to him.

In July 1296 the captured King John was taken to Montrose Castle. His symbols of **kingship** were confiscated and he was stripped of his **tabard** or jacket. This humiliating ceremony was usually performed on a disgraced knight found guilty of treason. King John became a prisoner of the English for years and was given the nickname of **Toom Tabard** or empty jacket.

The sack of Berwick

How did Edward take control?

- Scottish lords and nobles were forced to swear an **oath of loyalty**. Over 1500 leading Scots had to put their family **seal** on a piece of **parchment** on which the oath was written. This became known as the **Ragman Roll**.

- Edward took the **Stone of Destiny** from the Palace of Scone and had it placed underneath his own throne at Westminster Abbey in London. This stone had been used to crown the kings of Scotland for centuries.

- The official seal of the king of Scots was smashed up. All documents belonging to the Scottish king were taken to London.

- Edward's men stole one of the holiest **relics** in Scotland from Holyrood Abbey. The Black Rood of St Margaret was said to have been made from pieces of wood taken from the crucifix Christ died on.

- John de Warenne, Earl of Surrey, was made Governor of Scotland. Scottish castles were filled with English knights.

- Scots were **taxed** and the money collected was sent back to London.

Show your understanding

1. Write a sentence to explain why you think John Balliol was also called a puppet king by some nobles in Scotland.

2. Copy and complete the following table:

What Edward did	He did this because…	Scots would have felt…
Oath of loyalty signed and added onto the Ragman Roll		

3. Complete either a) or b).

   a) In pairs, make a series of flash cards about this section with questions on one side and answers on the other. You will show the answer to another pair and they have to guess what the question is. Rate the answers in terms of difficulty: 1 = easy, 4 = difficult.

   b) Create a Facebook page for King John Balliol and one for Edward I. Include key information as well as fun things such as 'nicknames', 'likes/dislikes' and 'pet hates'!

What is a rebellion?

What are we exploring?

By the end of this section you should be able to:

▶ Explain what a rebellion is

▶ Describe how William Wallace won and then lost his rebellion

▶ Imagine what would have happened if Wallace had won at Falkirk

Activate your brain cells!

- Do you always do as you are told? Discuss with a partner.
- Can you think of a time when it would be clever not to do what people tell you to do?
- Why might people in the past have rebelled?

By 1296 Scotland had joined with England, but Edward I did not know that the war to control Scotland had not ended – it had only just begun.

Who was William Wallace?

A **rebellion** happens when people go against their leaders. In Scotland, outraged men sought to drive out the English and bring John Balliol back as king. The most famous of these was William Wallace, a knight's son, who was made an **outlaw** when he would not promise to be loyal to Edward.

From all parts of Scotland, ordinary folk joined Wallace's rebellion. The men of the north-east joined under the leadership of the powerful and intelligent Andrew of Moray.

In September 1297, Wallace and Andrew Moray led their men to battle at **Stirling Bridge**. They destroyed the much larger English army, killing many lords and knights. Wallace was made **Guardian of Scotland** in 1298, keeping Scotland safe for King John Balliol, who was still a prisoner in England.

Victory at Stirling Bridge

SOURCE A

Source B

Wallace and Moray decided to fight the English at Stirling. They waited on the far side of the bridge over the River Forth and allowed some English soldiers to cross. Then they charged. The bridge was so narrow that only two knights could cross at a time so the English could not join the battle quickly. Some knights fell in the river and drowned.

Source C

Moray died from his wounds soon after the battle. I think Moray was the real reason the rebels won, not Wallace. Moray was certainly Wallace's equal and was a very clever leader in battle.

Source D

It could be argued that the reason the English lost the battle was that Edward I was not there. He was off fighting another war in France. The Earl of Surrey was not a good leader. Edward's experience would not have allowed the English to fall into Wallace's trap.

Source E

Some Scottish nobles actually fought for the English against the Scottish rebels. They wanted to keep their status and power. It is too simple to say that the battle was England versus Scotland.

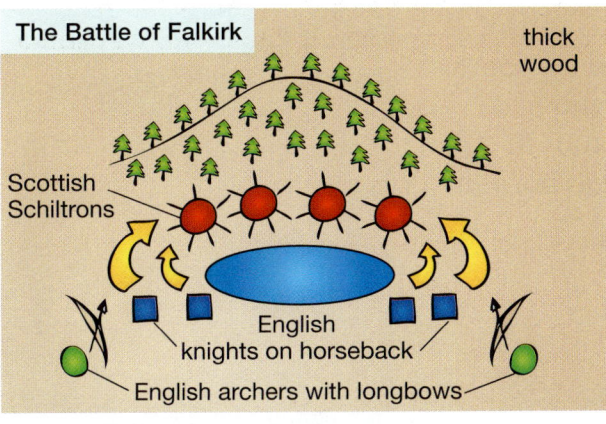

The Battle of Falkirk

thick wood

Scottish Schiltrons

English knights on horseback

English archers with longbows

Wallace is captured

Edward I returned from France in 1298 and headed to Scotland with a huge army and a powerful new weapon called the **longbow**. The English defeated Wallace's army at Falkirk and Wallace went on the run. In 1305 Wallace was **betrayed** by a Scottish noble and captured by the English. He was carried off to London, tried and executed as a traitor to Edward I and England. He was hung up until he was almost dead. Then his body was **drawn** (a form of **disembowelling**) and his remains were **quartered**. Pieces of his body were sent to be shown in Newcastle, Berwick, Perth and Stirling.

Show your understanding

1. Who was Wallace and why was he an enemy of the English King Edward?
2. Why do you think Wallace won the battle of Stirling Bridge?
3. Complete the battle report on the Battle of Falkirk. Use the diagram to help you.
4. What would have happened if Wallace had won at Falkirk? Share your ideas with a partner and then the rest of the class.
5. Why do you think Wallace's body was tortured and put on display?

The Battle of Falkirk

Wallace's army took up a strong defensive position with a thick _____ behind them and a small _____ in front of them. The spearmen were arranged in four 'hedgehog-like' circles called _____.

The _____ horsemen advanced. They split into two sections and each one moved around to attack the sides of the _____ army. The spearmen stood firm in their **schiltrons**, and the English knights could not get through them. However, the English _____ fired their arrows at the centre of the schiltrons. Many Scottish spearmen were _____ and the English knights were able to break through. The Scottish rebellion was over.

35 Does Robert the Bruce deserve to be called a hero?

What are we exploring?

By the end of this section you should be able to:

▶ Give your opinion on whether or not Robert the Bruce deserves to be called a hero

▶ Explain why there are different interpretations of people in the past

▶ Imagine different opinions people might have of you

 Activate your brain cells!

- Write three words someone close to you might use to describe your personality.
- Ask the person next to you to describe you in three words.
- Were there any differences? Why might this be?
- What problems might historians have when finding out what people in the past were really like?

In 1306, Robert de Brus or Bruce made himself king of Scots at a ceremony in Scone.

Long after his death he was called 'Good King Robert' and some see him as the greatest Scot in history. Others have said that Bruce should not have become king, that he was selfish and even that he was a murderer.

Robert the Bruce was a powerful **landowner** in the south-west of Scotland. His ancestors were Normans who had come up from England. The Bruce family had lands in Scotland and England. Historians think Bruce was born in Essex and had twice sworn loyalty to Edward I. He had even fought against Wallace at the Battle of Falkirk.

After Wallace was defeated by King Edward, Bruce became a guardian of Scotland along with John Comyn, Balliol's nephew and Bruce's biggest rival for the throne. Bruce agreed to a meeting with Comyn in 1306 at the Church of Greyfriars in Dumfries. In front of the high altar, Bruce stabbed Comyn to death. He had decided to risk everything and try to become king.

Source D – from a Scottish chronicle

Bruce has murdered an innocent man to become king and so Edward I has announced that Bruce is a criminal and an **outlaw**. Moreover, the Catholic Pope has stated that by killing Comyn on the altar, Bruce has committed an act of **sacrilege** and refuses to recognise Bruce as the rightful king of this nation.

Source F – from another historian

Bruce fought a brutal **civil war** against his Scottish enemies. In 1308 he tore apart the lands belonging to his enemy, the Earl of Buchan. The area was a desolate wasteland for years afterwards. He planned an invasion of Ireland that went terribly wrong in 1318, leading to the death of his own brother.

Source E – from a modern historian

Bruce fought a **guerrilla war** against Edward. He avoided full-scale battles. Instead he chose to ambush or attack the English army at night. In just six years, Bruce and his men had skilfully ousted the English army from Scotland. His biggest victory came at Bannockburn in 1314. When Bruce died in 1329 Scotland was a free, independent kingdom and was at peace with England.

The Battle of Bannockburn

Source G – from an Internet debate on the Battle of Bannockburn

Histo1314 fan: I think the Scots won at Bannockburn because of Bruce's clever and careful planning. He had his soldiers dig pits into the road to trap the English mounted knights. They put long sharpened stakes in the ground and small iron spikes called caltrops were sprinkled on the ground. The English warhorses could not cross these simple but brutal traps to get at the back of the Scots army.

Libby342: There are two or more sides to every story. I think a more important reason for Scotland winning was that, unlike his father, Edward II was not really a fighter. The English army were badly led, arrogant and not ready to fight Bruce. The English thought it would be easy to win but got caught out by the challenging marshy landscape of Bannockburn.

Collect a skill

Studying sources for interpretation

As you have found out, there are different **interpretations** of Robert the Bruce. He was a complex person, as we all are.

1. Add the word interpretation and other words found here to your vocabulary list.
2. Why do you think there are different interpretations of people?

Show your understanding

1. Read **sources A** to **G**. List the reasons why Robert the Bruce could be called a hero. Then list the reasons why he might not be.
2. Does Robert the Bruce deserve to be called a hero? Explain your answer.
3. What does the term 'two sides to every story' mean?
4. Design a poster for a movie about Robert the Bruce. What scenes from his life will you show? Will you show him as a good king, a bad man or something else? Include statements about his life.

Who should be in charge of a country?

By the end of this section you should be able to:

▶ Name the most famous document in Scottish history

▶ Describe what it said

▶ Imagine what it has meant for Scotland ever since

In 1320, Scottish nobles wrote three letters to the **Pope**. The last of these letters is the most famous document in Scottish history. It is called the **Declaration of Arbroath**, and it argues that **freedom** is the best thing a country can have.

 Activate your brain cells!

- What does it mean to be free? Write a definition with a partner.
- When do you feel free? List as many ideas as you can and share them.
- Imagine if you were not free. What emotions would you feel?

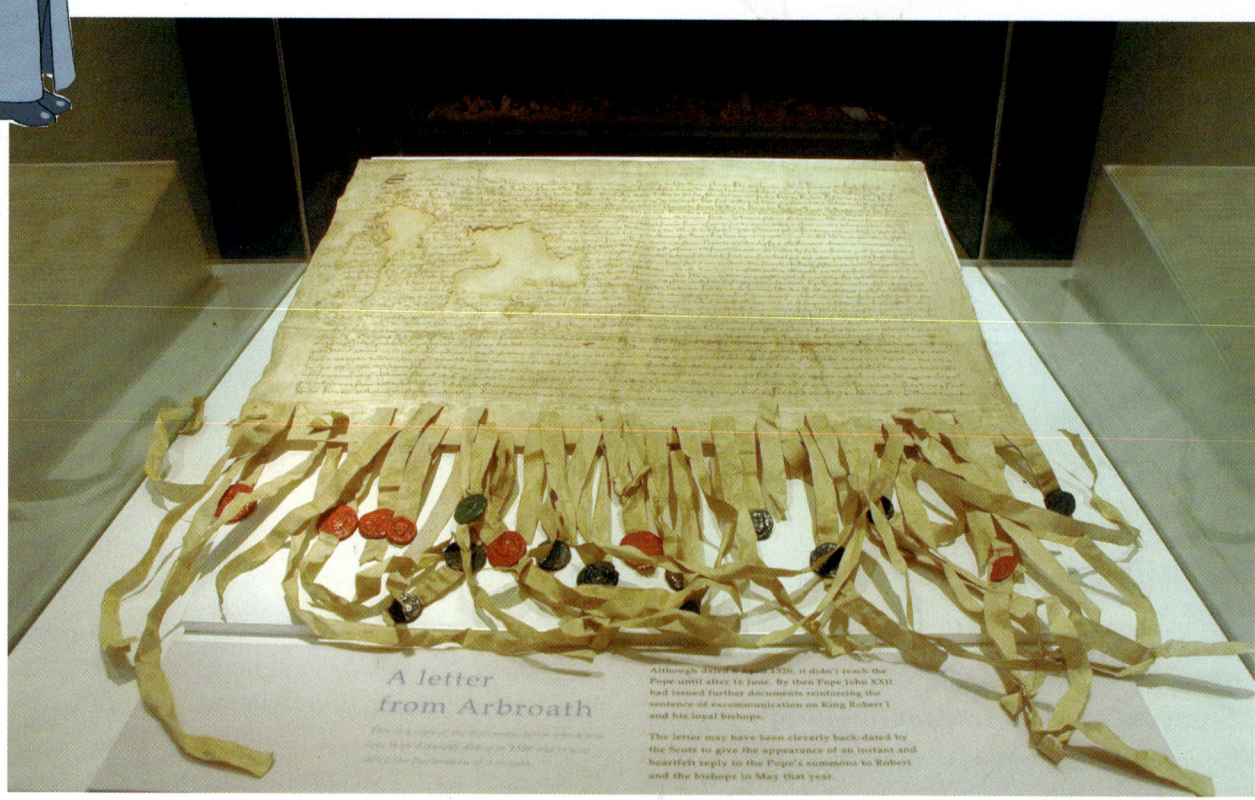

A letter from Arbroath

Why was it written?

The Catholic Church refused to accept Robert the Bruce as the king of Scotland. They knew that Bruce had murdered Comyn in a church and accused him of **sacrilege**.

Pope John XXII **excommunicated** Bruce in 1319. This meant that he no longer had the support of the Catholic Church. The Pope told Scottish Catholics to go against their king. He also banned Scottish priests from carrying out official services like baptisms or burials.

The Scottish nobles wrote three letters to the Pope hoping to persuade him that Bruce was the rightful king of Scots. The last of these letters was signed and sealed at Arbroath Abbey on 6 April 1320. The declaration said that all the people of Scotland accepted Bruce as their king. It argued that Scotland had always been free and that the English were to blame for the Wars of Independence. The most important paragraph is shown below:

> We support King Robert because he is the person who has given the people safety and freedom.
>
> But if he (King Robert the Bruce) were to give up the work he has begun, or wish to bring us or our kingdom under the rule of the king of the English or the English people, we would at once try to drive him out as our enemy … and we would choose another king to rule over us.
>
> For so long as one hundred men remain alive, we shall never submit to the rule of the English. It is not for glory, or riches, or honours that we fight, but for freedom alone, which no good man will give up except with his life.

 ## Show your understanding

Read the Declaration out loud to a partner then discuss the following questions:

1. Why did the nobles who signed the declaration support King Robert?
2. What do the nobles mean by 'we would choose another king to rule over us'? Who is in charge here – the king or his people? Is this different from what has gone before? How had kings been chosen previously?
3. How would they select another king? What would they do with Bruce? What problems might they face if they had to do this?
4. Write a sentence or two explaining why you think the last two sentences have become so famous among Scottish people.
5. This is the seal of Robert the Bruce. Each family had their own seal. In pairs, design your own seals to represent your noble families. Make several copies of them.
6. Plan and make a version of the Declaration of Arbroath. Collect seals from the rest of your class to attach on the bottom. Why were these seals attached?

 ### Explore further

Research more about the Wars of Independence, looking at some of these areas:

- the role of the nobles – whose side were they on?
- the Battle of Stirling Bridge
- the Battle of Falkirk
- the Battle of Bannockburn
- the schiltron
- the longbow
- historical errors in the film *Braveheart*
- the reign of Robert the Bruce
- the Declaration of Arbroath.

What was the Renaissance?

What are we exploring?

By the end of this section you should be able to:

▶ Explain what and when the Renaissance was

▶ Describe the importance of the printing press

▶ Imagine how new ways of thinking changed the world forever

We live in a world that is constantly changing. In 1903 Orville Wright's tiny aircraft flew for 12 seconds. In 1969 Neil Armstrong walked on the Moon. Now we can communicate instantly with people around the world using the Internet and mobile phones.

It is difficult to imagine living in a society where little changes, but that was what life was like in Europe at the beginning of the fifteenth century. It was about to change forever.

Activate your brain cells!

• Have you ever invented something?

• With a partner, write down famous inventions you know about.

• What does the latest mobile phone look like and do? Why is it better than the last one?

From 1450 there was an explosion of ideas and discoveries across Europe. For the next three centuries, Europeans had new thoughts and discoveries in science, medicine, engineering, painting, sculpture, music, mathematics and writing. This very important **era** is known as the '**Renaissance**'. The French word renaissance means to be 'reborn'.

How did it start?

During the Middle Ages all books had to be handwritten by monks and they were mostly bibles, prayer books or religious stories. It took a long time to handwrite books and so they were rare and expensive. Few people could get their hands on one and few people needed to be able to read.

Around 1450, a German called Johannes Gutenburg spread black ink onto a few wooden blocks with letters carved on them. He arranged the blocks and pressed them onto paper to print a word. Gutenburg had invented the printing press.

As more books were published, more people wanted to read. It became fashionable to write books as well as read them. Soon there were books on travel, hunting, fishing, medicine and different religions.

For years, people had accepted that the Bible had all the answers to their questions. Now educated people began to read the books written by the Greeks and Romans who lived before Christ. They found to their amazement that these civilisations knew a lot more than people had realised.

Across Europe scientists, writers, mathematicians and doctors began to ask questions and look for better ways of doing things.

What did 'Renaissance Man' look like?

Leonardo Da Vinci sums up everything about the Renaissance. He was determined to be the best at everything he did and he was into everything! From science to art, astronomy to architecture, Da Vinci studied hard hoping to discover new ways of doing things. He was a true Renaissance Man.

Da Vinci thought of hundreds of study ideas years before anyone else. Here are some of his sketches and a few of his ideas:

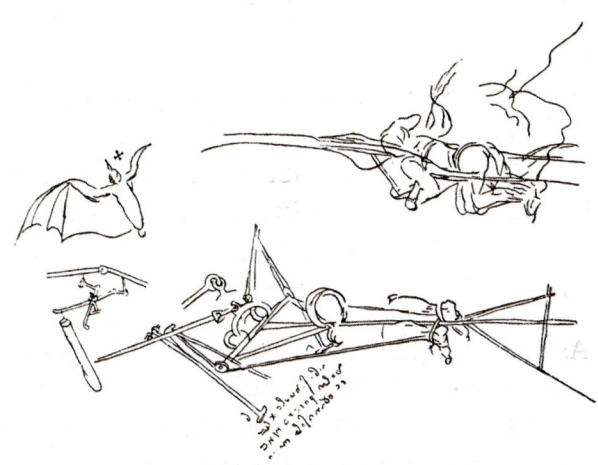

- the human embryo
- fossils
- oil painting (the *Mona Lisa*)
- glass making
- weapon building
- flying machines
- tanks
- canals
- lifebelts
- submarines

Show your understanding

1. Write a sentence or two to explain what the word Renaissance means.
2. Write a paragraph explaining how the printing press was invented and why it was so important for human society. Try to include the following words: **invention / communication / books / text / reading**.
3. If someone today was called a modern 'Renaissance' type of person, what would they be like? What sort of things would they be interested in?
4. Create a table showing Da Vinci's ideas. Illustrate your list and write a sentence or two explaining why his ideas are important to us today.

Idea	Drawing	Why is it important for us today?

5. Choose to answer either a) or b).
   a) **Printing time!** In groups, make your own printing press blocks out of wood or polystyrene. Create words by putting the letters together. Ink them up and print onto paper to make a word or sentence.
   b) **Be like Leonardo** – think of something that would make your life easier and design it:
   - pitch your ideas to the rest of the class and your teacher – they can choose to invest in the best three inventions.

How did Europe discover the world?

What are we exploring?

By the end of this section you should be able to:

► Explain why the explorers set off to find new countries
► Name and talk about some important explorers
► Imagine what life would be like if they had not explored at all

Activate your brain cells!

- Name a country in the world you would you like to visit and explain to your partner why.
- Plan how you will get there. What transport will you take? How easy will it be? What will you need?

Few ordinary people in the Middle Ages travelled once they had settled somewhere. Those that did travel brought back fearful tales of robbers and outlaws, pirates and unknown lands full of bizarre creatures and ferocious monsters.

As travel technology improved, **merchants** carried their goods increasingly long distances to sell them. They traded gold, precious stones and spices. Some merchants began trading humans as slaves.

In the late Middle Ages the **monarchs** of France, Spain, Portugal and Britain wanted to find gold, silver and spices to increase their wealth. Some employed men to explore in their name. Their discoveries increased the power and **prestige** of monarchs and helped to build their **empires**.

Some great voyages of discovery

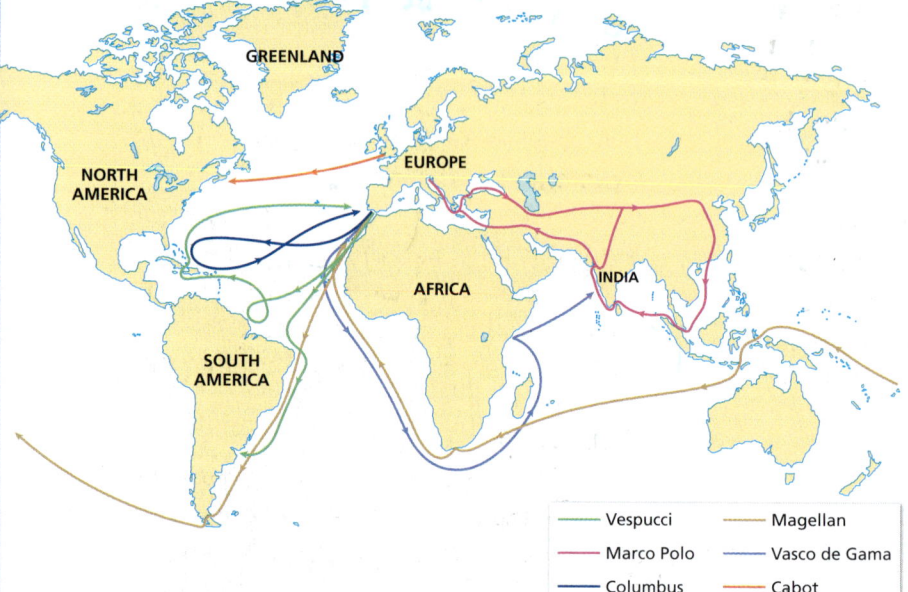

New ideas and new horizons

Marco Polo

Marco Polo was probably Europe's first great explorer. In 1262 he travelled from Venice to trade along the silk road. He reached the court of the Mongol leader, Kublai Khan. Polo made many **diplomatic** missions for Khan. He saw lots of China before returning to Venice.

Christopher Columbus

In 1490 the only way to reach China was to travel east along the spice route. Columbus was sure that he could reach China, India and the 'Spice Islands' of the east by sailing west. He spotted land on 12 October 1492 and went ashore. He kidnapped locals and took them as presents for Queen Isabella of Spain. He also took gold, herbs, fish and a parrot!

Columbus was convinced he had found a new route to India. In fact, the islands he discovered were called the West Indies. Columbus died in 1506 unaware that he had discovered a new continent, **America**.

John Cabot

In 1497 the Italian explorer set off from Bristol to try to reach Asia by sailing north-west. He sailed to Canada, where he named and explored the coast of **Newfoundland**.

Vasco De Gama

This Portuguese explorer proved in 1498 that it was possible to reach India by sailing around the bottom of Africa and up the eastern coast.

Amerigo Vespucci

From 1499 to 1503, this Spanish explorer continued to explore the seas Columbus had sailed. Some historians think America was named after him.

Ferdinand Magellan

On 20 September 1519, five Portuguese ships led by Magellan set off aiming to sail around the world. Magellan died on the voyage but one ship and 18 men made it home in 1522. Their journey took them to the tip of South America and round to the Pacific – which he named.

Show your understanding

1 Use string to make a world map on the floor. Now use different coloured string or tape to mark out the journeys of the explorers on the map.
2 Which journey of discovery do you think was the most important? Write down why and share it with a partner.
3 Explorers were big celebrities at the time. Some were treated as heroes. Why do you think this was?
4 Choose to answer either a) or b).
   a) Design a computer game about the six explorers. How could it be played? How would their ships be controlled? What would the locals do when they meet them? Storyboard the action.
   b) Imagine you have just interviewed the celebrity explorer Chris Columbus! What was he like? What stories did he tell?

39 Who lived in the New World?

What are we exploring?

By the end of this section you should be able to:

▶ Explain what the Aztec civilization was like

▶ Describe the purpose of human sacrifice in Aztec society

▶ Imagine what Europeans at the time thought about the Aztecs

Explorers nicknamed the Americas 'the New World' because it was a world of new opportunities and promises of wealth.

In February 1519 the Spanish explorer Hernan Cortés marched his 600 **conquistador** troops across Central America. They defeated **natives** using guns, horses, steel swords and armour.

When Cortés reached the centre of what is now called Mexico he was amazed by the civilisation he found there. It was a land of gold, precious stones and strange people with gruesome religious ceremonies. He had found the **Aztec Empire**.

What was the Aztec civilisation like?

The capital of the Aztec kingdom was **Tenochtitlan**, built on a lake. It was bigger than any city in Europe at the time – as many as 300,000 people lived there.

Tenochtitlan

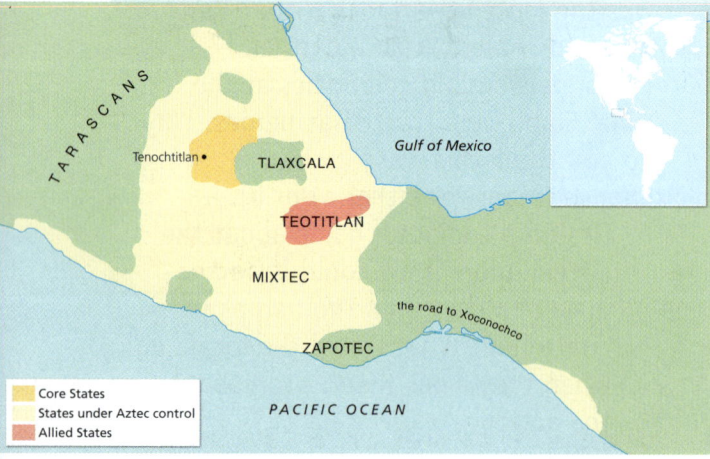

The New World and the Aztec Empire

TARASCANS

Tenochtitlan •
TLAXCALA

Gulf of Mexico

TEOTITLAN

MIXTEC

the road to Xoconochco

ZAPOTEC

PACIFIC OCEAN

Core States
States under Aztec control
Allied States

Activate your brain cells!

- Draw a picture or make a model showing where you will be in five years' time if everything goes really well.
- Successful people think about the best that could happen, not the worst. Which bits of your picture are most important to you? Why? What would make you most proud?
- Why might some people want to make a 'new start' in a 'new world'?

Source A – written in Cortés' diary in 1520

Great towns and cities rise from the water, all made of stone – like a fairytale. It is all so wonderful; we have seen things never dreamt of. We have also seen horrors. Thousands of people killed, their hearts ripped out in sacrifice at the altar on top of their huge pyramid.

Source B – from a lecture on the Aztec religion

The Aztecs worshipped hundreds of gods. These gods looked after areas of human life. Sacrifices were made to the Sun gods in the hope of good weather for growing crops. The Aztecs respected the power of their gods and avoided angering them by offering up the most valuable gift – human life.

Source C – part of an investigation by Cortés' General

The people of Tenochtitlan are farmers. They are given land to farm once they get married. They grow corn, beans, peppers and squash. There are no sheep, cows or horses but people keep birds called turkeys, as well as rabbits and ducks for food.

Source D – the notes kept by Cortés' doctor

Life is different here. People get up as soon as it is light. Priests beat drums and blow trumpets to celebrate the coming of the Sun gods. Meat is not eaten unless it is a special occasion. Ordinary people wear simple clothes. Nobles wear richly embroidered cotton and the priests wear vibrant colours and lots of gold. All boys go to school. The sons of rich people go to boarding schools called **calmecac**, where they are taught history, medicine and astrology by priests.

Source E – from an archaeological study

They did not have an alphabet like we do. They wrote in **glyphs** that were drawn according to strict rules. Aztecs needed a lot of training to be able to read and write them. Books were made of sheets of bark paper or deerskin folded like an accordion.

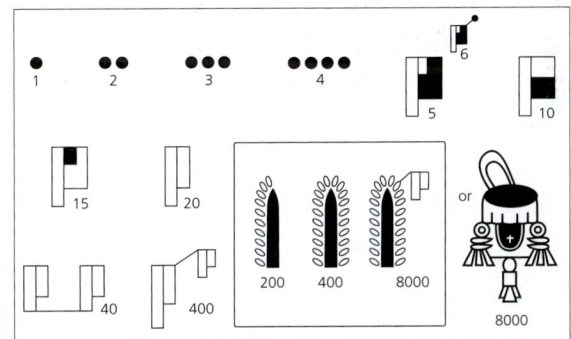

🧩 Show your understanding

1 Read Source A. How might you feel about the Aztecs if you were Cortés?

2 Copy and complete the following table for Sources A–E.

Source	What it says (brief summary)	Primary or secondary?	Who wrote it?	Why is it a good source for finding out about the Aztecs?
Source A				

3 The picture above shows how the Aztecs wrote numbers. Can you write out the numbers 1 to 30 in the way the Aztecs would have done?

4 Write out the following numbers: 8000 16,000 25 600 45

How does a society disappear?

What are we exploring?

By the end of this section you should be able to:

▶ Explain why the Aztecs and Incas died out
▶ Describe the advantages that the Spanish conquerors had
▶ Argue for or against the idea that Cortés was a killer

The ruins of an Aztec temple

Cortés' troops destroy the city of Tenochtitlan

By 1570 the Spanish **conquistadors** controlled a large area of land in the New World, including the Aztecs and the Inca people of Peru. Within a few years, the conquistadors managed to take over and destroy the most powerful civilisations and replaced those empires with **plantations** and gold and silver mines.

In Mexico, Cortés killed the Aztec Emperor Montezuma and had his troops demolish the great city of Tenochtitlan. Many Aztecs died in the fighting and later from hunger and disease.

Why did the Aztec and Inca peoples die out?

The Spanish were able to conquer the Aztecs and the Incas because they had great advantages.

Activate your brain cells!

- The Earth is being invaded by aliens! What types of weapons do they have? Be as creative as you like!
- Can you think of any problems humans might have fighting against them?
- Look at the ruins of the Aztec temple. What has happened to all the people?

Conquistador weapons and armour

The Spanish brought with them diseases that attacked the **native** population. The Spanish soldiers were used to smallpox and influenza and had some immunity to them, but Native Americans had never experienced those diseases before. This made it much more likely that they would catch diseases from the Spanish. There were around 21 million Aztecs in 1519 but they had shrunk to 2.5 million by 1565 and just 1 million by 1607. In Peru just 1.5 million people remained where there had once been 11 million.

The Spanish had much better technology. The Inca and Aztecs were armed with bows and spears, but the Spanish had muskets and cannons. To people who had never seen horses or a metal army, and had never seen gunpowder, the shining Spanish army must have been quite a fearful sight. Some of the Incas and Aztecs thought they were fighting gods or demons.

The Aztecs were a cruel people themselves. They were happy to abuse Native American Indians as slaves. Aztecs had also violently attacked their neighbours. So it did not take the Spanish much convincing to get those neighbours to help them to destroy the Aztec Empire.

 Show your understanding

1 Write a sentence or two to explain why the conquistadors destroyed the Aztec and Inca civilisations.
2 The diseases brought by the Spanish became known as the 'White Deaths'. Can you explain how they got this name?
3 Draw a simple line graph showing the changes in population in Mexico from 1519 to 1607.
4 What does this graph tell you about the speed of the decline of the Aztec people?
5 Songs are a great way of telling a story and have often been used to talk about the people of the past. Use the Internet to find the lyrics to the song 'Cortés the

Killer' by Neil Young. It was written in 1975. Listen to the song if you can. What does Neil Young think of Cortés? What does he think about the Aztecs?
6 Choose to answer either a) or b).
   a) Write your own song lyrics to explain what happened to the Aztecs. Think of a melody if you can! What instruments will you play your song on?
   b) What is your opinion of the conquistadors and the Aztecs? Write a paragraph explaining what you think of them both. Try to be as **balanced** in your argument as possible.

Who were the fathers of the United States of America?

What are we exploring?

By the end of this section you should be able to:

▶ Explain who the Pilgrim Fathers were

▶ Describe how they survived their first few years in America

▶ Imagine how different life would be if the Pilgrim Fathers had failed

Every 25 November, millions of Americans have a day off work and sit down to a meal of turkey or goose, cranberry sauce and pumpkin pie. It sounds a bit like Christmas but it's not! It is a day when Americans remember the first settlers of their country.

In 1607 an Englishman called John Smith led a group of people aiming to set up a **colony** called Jamestown in North America. No other Europeans had set up a colony in the Americas before.

⚙ Activate your brain cells!

- In pairs, list as many things made in the USA as you can. Add them to a class list.
- In what ways is Britain similar to the USA? How much influence does the USA have on our lives?
- In what ways is Britain different from the USA?

Source A – John Smith describes meeting the native Americans for the first time

We had not seen the locals until the third day. Then three of them appeared in a little boat. One of them came aboard. He spoke a strange language to us without any sign of fear. We gave him a shirt, a hat, wine and meat. He seemed to like our gifts. Then he went away in his own boat. Within half an hour he had filled his boat with fish, which he came and shared with us.

On 6 September 1620, 102 people left England for a new life in Smith's colony. Thirty-five of them were **Puritans** who led strict Christian lives by following the word of the Bible and keeping free from sin. The group sailed for over two months in a small ship called *The Mayflower*.

On 11 November, they finally reached land. There they built a new settlement and called it **Plymouth**, after the place from which they had set sail. They planned to survive by eating fish caught from the sea, but by the spring of 1621 half of them had died of starvation or disease.

The success of the Puritan **pilgrims** encouraged more British, French and Dutch settlers. The Dutch built a colony called **New Amsterdam**, which later became New York.

Quickly the English began to take control of more and more land in North America. Products from America such as tobacco, sugar and cotton began to be taken back to Europe and sold, making many people on both sides of the Atlantic Ocean very rich.

The Mayflower landed here, at what is now called Cape Cod. Why was this bay a good place to settle?

Source B – William Bradford, from his book *History of the Plymouth Plantation (1651)*

The Plymouth settlers had no friends to welcome them, no inns to entertain or refresh their weather-beaten bodies, no houses to stay in. They faced a cold and stormy winter, and had to put up with cruel and fierce storms. All they could see was a wild and empty land, full of wild beasts and wild men.

Source C – an extract from a modern History textbook

A local tribesman called Squanto showed the settlers how to plant corn and barley correctly. He used dead fish to **fertilise** the soil. The settlers were taught how to farm properly and life started to improve. To celebrate their good harvests and give thanks to God they had a feast of turkey and goose.

Show your understanding

1 Write a sentence or two to describe how the locals treated the first settlers.
2 Who were the Puritans? How do you think they got their name?
3 What problems did the settlers of *The Mayflower* come up against? Use the text and **Sources B** and **C** to help you.
4 According to **Source C**, what does Thanksgiving Day celebrate?
5 Complete either a) or b).
   a) Copy the picture of *The Mayflower* onto a map and illustrate the ship's journey. Show all the things you would have taken with you if you were one of the Puritans on board. You cannot take anything that was invented after 1620!
   b) In groups, plan and act out a series of still photographs to tell the story of the Pilgrim Fathers.

What was the Reformation?

What are we exploring?

By the end of this section you should be able to:

▶ Explain what the Reformation was

▶ Describe the differences between the Protestant and Catholic faiths

▶ Imagine why these differences cause tension today

 Activate your brain cells!

- Can you remember the last time you were in a church? Tell your partner why you were there.
- Imagine everyone went to church on a Sunday. What would your community be like?
- Other than Celtic and Rangers, what do you know about Catholics and Protestants?

By 1500 most Europeans were Catholics. They used God to explain things they didn't understand: if their **harvest** was bad, it was because God wished it to be; heaven and hell were thought to be real places.

In the sixteenth century, some people tried to change the Catholic religion. They wanted to make it better than they believed it was. They wanted to **reform** it. These changes can be called the **Reformation**.

Who was Martin Luther?

Luther had been a monk and then a professor at the German University of Wittenberg. He hated what he saw as the greedy and lazy attitudes of many Catholics. In 1517 he made a list of all the things he thought were wrong with the Catholic church and nailed them to his front door for his neighbours to read. You can read his list below.

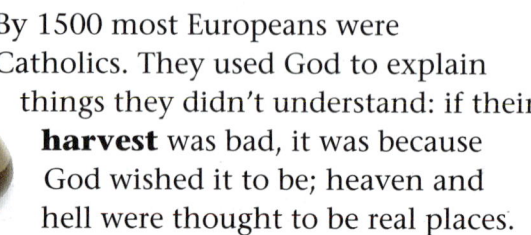

- Travelling holy **con-men** called 'Pardoners' make lots of money by persuading people that they can buy forgiveness for their sins. They also sell fake holy **relics** – objects that are supposed to have once belonged to Jesus or one of his saints.
- Churchmen make too much money from the land given to their church by the king. Every year a peasant farmer has to pay up to a tenth of all the produce from his land and flocks to the church.
- Ordinary people cannot understand much of what is said during mass. The Bible is written in Latin and the church services are held mainly in this language as well.

After making his public protest, Luther was sent a letter from the Pope **expelling** him from the Catholic faith. He burnt the Pope's letter in the middle of a market place!

Luther spent the next few years in hiding but his ideas for a reform of the church spread across Europe. His followers became known as **Protestants** because they protested against the Catholic religion.

Who was John Calvin?

A young Frenchman called John Calvin heard Luther's ideas and added that services should be simpler, as they were in the early days of Christianity. He complained that church buildings had become a grand show of gold and images. He said that churches should lose all displays of wealth and have simple blank walls.

Calvin believed that there should be no bishops; the worshippers at each church should choose their own rulers. This sort of church is called **Presbyterian**. In the end, the followers of Luther and Calvin set up their own form of Christian religion and they became known as the **Protestant Reformers**. For the next 600 years, Catholics and Protestants often argued and sometimes fought violently.

 Show your understanding

1. Why was the Catholic religion so powerful in 1500? Explain to a partner.
2. Write a short paragraph explaining what Luther said was wrong with the Catholic religion in 1517.
3. How did the Protestants get their name?
4. Who chose the leaders of Calvin's Presbyterian churches? Do you think this was a good or bad idea? Explain your answer.
5. Write out the following statements and decide which describe the Catholic religion and which describe the Protestant religion:
   - The Pope is head of the church and is chosen by God.
   - A church should be a bright and colourful place to worship God.
   - The king or queen of the country is head of the church.
   - Churches should have pictures on walls, stained glass windows, silver cups and a large stone altar.
   - Money should not be wasted on decorations or robes for the priest.
   - The Bible and prayer books are written in Latin.
   - The Bible should be in a language that worshippers understand, not in Latin.
   - A church should be a plain and simple place.

43 Why was Mary's life such a tragedy?

What are we exploring?

By the end of this section you should be able to:

▶ Describe important events in Mary's life
▶ Explain the problems Mary posed for Elizabeth I of England
▶ Argue for or against Elizabeth's decision to execute Mary

 Activate your brain cells!

- We have a limited lifetime – what could you plan now for your future?
- If you became king or queen, how would you feel about your future?

In 1560 a new queen of Scotland arrived from France. Few crowds gathered to welcome her. Scotland was a Protestant country; Mary was Catholic.

Many folk in Edinburgh did not like the dancing, music and merrymaking they heard coming from nineteen year-old Mary's palace in Holyrood. They liked the Catholic mass that was said in her chapel even less. Protestant John Knox did his best to change her religion but she refused to change.

In 1565 Mary married Lord Darnley, another Catholic. He was unpopular amongst Scottish lords, often drunk and bad tempered. There were also rumours that Mary was having an affair with her secretary, David Rizzio.

In March 1566, Rizzio was murdered by Darnley and his friends in front of a pregnant Mary. Three months later Mary's son, James, was born. By now Mary despised Darnley and had fallen in love with another – the Earl of Bothwell.

Mary Queen of Scots

Who killed Darnley?

In February 1567, the peace of Edinburgh was shattered by an explosion in buildings attached to the Kirk O'Field. The body of Darnley was found in the garden. He had been strangled.

Some nobles accused Bothwell and Mary of being involved as Bothwell's servant had been found at the scene. Bothwell took Mary to Dunbar Castle because he said she was in 'grave danger'. They married less than a month later.

Mary gives up her crown

The Scottish nobles rebelled in 1567, forcing Mary to **abdicate**. Her infant son became King James VI of Scotland. Mary fled to England hoping her cousin, Queen Elizabeth I, would protect her. Instead, she was arrested and put in prison.

How do you solve a problem like Mary?

Many people in England didn't want Elizabeth to support Mary. The English parliament worried that she was involved in a plot to kill Elizabeth and wanted to execute her. Here is a list of arguments that Elizabeth considered:

- In 1586, spies claimed they had found evidence that Mary had been involved in plots against Elizabeth and also in the murder of Darnley. Elizabeth didn't really believe the evidence – it may have come from forgery or trickery.

- Elizabeth was getting old and had no children. Mary and her son James were next in line to the English throne.

- Mary said she knew nothing about the plots against Elizabeth.

- Mary was Catholic and threatened the English Protestant Church.

- The English parliament wanted Mary to be put to death.

- Mary was a monarch, supposedly chosen by God. Would executing her go against God?

- Mary was Scottish, so technically she couldn't be tried by an English court.

- As long as Mary was alive, Catholic plots against Elizabeth would continue.

- Mary had written to powerful people abroad and asked for their help to escape.

As plot after plot was uncovered, Elizabeth could delay no further. In 1587, after 19 years in captivity, Mary was put on trial. She was found guilty and sentenced to death. Early on a February morning at Fotheringay Castle, Mary walked calmly and quietly to her execution.

Show your understanding

1. Do you think Mary had any regrets about her life? Discuss with a partner.
2. Choose a moment in Mary's life and write a Tweet about 'what's happening' to post on Twitter. Messages must be a maximum of 140 characters so you have to select your words wisely!
3. What choices did Elizabeth have in dealing with Mary? Arrange Elizabeth's arguments into a table like this one:

Execute Mary	Save Mary

4. What do you think Elizabeth should have done? Explain your answer.
5. Complete either a) or b).
   a) Design a cartoon strip about Mary's life. Include a detailed description of the events.
   b) In groups, make an animation or a play of an event in Mary's life.

Early modern Britain

What is a civil war?

What are we exploring?

By the end of this section you should be able to:

► Explain what a civil war is

► Describe how civil war tore Britain apart

► Imagine what would happen if civil war broke out in Britain today

Royalists versus Parliamentarians

For several years, King James VI of Scotland (James I of England) argued with parliament. His son continued to argue when he became King Charles I in 1625. Both men believed parliament should obey the king. However, parliament thought the king should serve the country. This argument was about who should have the most power in Britain.

On 22 August 1642, Charles declared war against his enemies in the English parliament. This led to men fighting over whether they supported the king or the parliament. Fathers fought against their sons and brothers fought against each other. This **civil war** divided Britain.

On one side were Charles and his followers, known as the Royalists or **Cavaliers**. On the other side were the men of parliament

Activate your brain cells!

• Have you ever argued about a really important issue with a friend or family member? How did you fix things? List five top tips for making peace after an argument.

and their followers, known as the Parliamentarians or **Roundheads**.

In June 1642, Cromwell (parliament) and Charles began preparing for war. In June 1645 the Parliamentarians defeated the Royalists at the Battle of Naseby and Charles I was taken prisoner.

Parliament decided a king was no longer necessary. Oliver Cromwell ruled England, calling himself the **Lord Protector**. Cromwell wanted everyone to live like Puritans. He had all pubs and theatres closed down. Sport was banned and he even stopped people celebrating Christmas!

*God has made me king. This means I have a **divine** (God-given) right to do as I please. Parliament thinks it can control me by keeping money from me. Parliament must be stopped… even if it means a civil war.*

King Charles I

We have been helping kings and queens for years and they have taken us for granted. Charles I only uses us to gather taxes from the people. When we last refused to give Charles I any tax money, he closed parliament and sent us home for 11 years! He was forced to ask us back because he needed us to raise money for an army to fight the Scots. They invaded because of his stubborn ways. He told them to use a Bible they didn't like. He has to be stopped… even if it means war. We propose nineteen demands to give parliament more control. You are either with us or with the king.

Oliver Cromwell, a member of the English parliament

We Covenanters are determined to continue the Protestant Reformation in Scotland. Charles told us to use a new prayer book. He is meddling in Scottish religious affairs and must be stopped.

Scottish Covenanter

Our pure way of worship is more popular than ever before. Many of us are members of parliament. Charles has married a young Catholic princess and is causing trouble in Ireland – is he trying to make our country more Catholic?

A Scottish Puritan

Charles has put me in prison because I've refused to pay his ship money. He has taxed imports to pay for an army to go to Scotland and force them to use the English prayer book. The English army was defeated by the Scots and Charles foolishly agreed to pay Scotland £850 per day until the matter was settled. Money he did not have! We now have to pay two taxes. I won't do it.

An English merchant, John Hampden

In 1660, Charles II was **restored** as king of England. The men who had signed his father's death warrant were tried as **regicides** (murderers of a king) and executed. Anyone linked with Charles I's death was put on trial.

An eyewitness to Charles' execution on 30 January 1649

The executioner refused to kill the king. When a willing executioner was found, he was allowed to wear a mask so no one knew who he was. Charles looked calm. I heard that he had asked to wear thick underclothes as he was very concerned that if he shivered in the cold, the crowd might think that he was scared. His last words were: 'I pray God you do the right things for the good of the kingdom and your own salvation. I die a **martyr**. I die for the good of the people of England.' When he was beheaded, thousands began wailing. I've never heard such a cry and I never want to hear one like it again. I wasn't sad for the traitor though.

Show your understanding

1. Write a sentence to describe what the term 'civil war' means.
2. How did the civil war affect ordinary families?
3. Use the information in the five speech bubbles to compile a list of arguments for supporting the Royalists and a list of arguments for supporting the Parliamentarians.
4. Why do you think people cried when Charles I was executed? Draw a cartoon of the crowd scene on 30 January 1649.

45 Why did Scotland unite with England in 1707?

What are we exploring?

By the end of this section you should be able to:

▶ Explain why Scotland joined with England

▶ Imagine what might have happened if the agreement was not signed

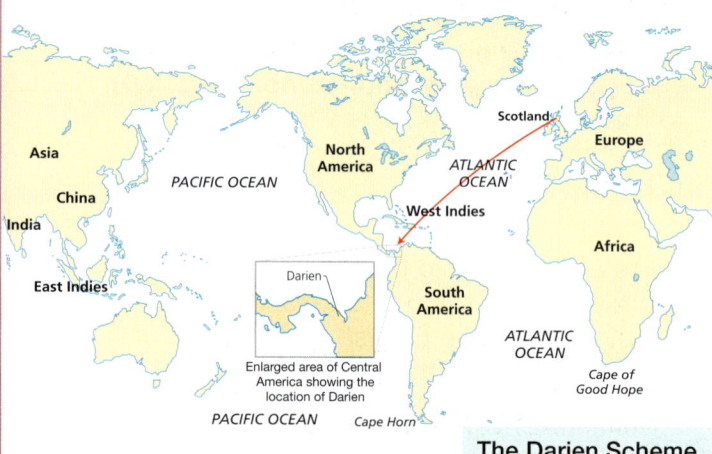

The Darien Scheme

Activate your brain cells!

- If you're British, are you Scottish, English, Welsh or Irish?
- What does being British mean? Is it different from the terms above?
- Can you name another country that is made up of several other countries?
- Imagine Scotland wasn't part of Britain. What be would the good and bad points?

Source A – extract from a historian's book about the 'Darien Scheme' (2001)

In 1706, Scotland had no money. The disastrous Darien Scheme was a complete and utter failure and led directly to the Union.

Scotland's nobles borrowed and invested £400,000 trying to start Scotland's empire in Central America. Scots settlers were met by hostile natives. They also suffered extreme heat and disease. Supplies ran out and the Spanish took control of the whole area.

King William of England refused to help the Scots despite being fierce rivals of Spain. He thought that if Darien succeeded, Scotland might begin to challenge England's financial strength. Over 2000 settlers died.

Source B – extract from the diary of a Scottish minister in March 1707

Darien investors like me need our money back. Scotland has to find £398,000 from somewhere. England has offered this sum of money and has called it the **'Equivalent'**. In return, Scotland must join a Union with England.

Source C – from the BBC History website

The Union was not about England rescuing a bankrupt and poor Scotland. The nobles thought Scotland was ruined. In fact, Scottish overseas trade was still very strong. In the four months before the Union, Scottish investors put £300,000 in brandies, wines, salt and whalebones. They intended to export these to England tax-free after 1 May.

Source D – from www.highlanderrants.com

The Scottish politicians were not corrupt, they were simply useless. They negotiated the terms of the treaty and gave in too easily. England was prepared to offer much more, but the Scots settled too quickly. The nobles panicked and agreed that they should raise Scottish taxes to English levels. So we Scots basically paid our own way out of the financial crisis without England's help!

Source E – from an English textbook

England had to quickly secure a Treaty of Union with Scotland. She was fighting a war with France at the time. England could not allow the possibility of Scotland joining forces with France and attacking from the north. Any treaty would also make Scotland pay towards the cost of the war with France.

Source F – from the diary of a Scottish noble in April 1707

England is bullying us. It has banned all trade from us unless we sign the treaty. Their 'Aliens Act' takes away my right to my own lands and property in England. The English army is at the border between our countries. We must sign.

Rules of Union

- Scotland and England become the **United Kingdom**.
- Rulers of the UK to be **Protestant** Hanoverians (not Scots Stuarts).
- **No Catholic** can ever become king or queen of the UK.
- Parliament to be in **London** – Edinburgh parliament closed.
- **Sixteen** Scottish lords and **196** English lords in the UK parliament.
- **Forty-five** Scottish MPs and **513** English MPs in the UK parliament.
- Scotland will keep its own legal system and its own church.

Show your understanding

1. Which of the following factors do you think was the most important in the Union of 1707? Explain your answer.
   - Scotland had no money because of the Darien failure.
   - The English army was ready to invade Scotland if nobles did not sign the treaty.
   - The Scots nobles were poor politicians who panicked into signing.
   - The Scots nobles sold Scotland for English gold.
2. Design an alternative union flag commemorating the 1707 Union.

Collect a skill

Who wrote it and why did they bother?

Knowing who wrote a source or why it was published can give us important clues as to whether what they are saying is biased or exaggerated. You can use this skill throughout your life – don't believe everything you read!

- Copy and complete the table to help you investigate who wrote the sources.

Source	Who wrote it?	Where did they write it?	Why did they write it?	Should you trust the author? Why?	How much I trust the author (1 = highest / 7 = lowest)
A	A historian in 2001	In a book	To sell books. To seek the truth about people in the past.		

Who were the Jacobites?

What are we exploring?	**By the end of this section you should be able to:**

- ▶ Explain what the Jacobites fought for
- ▶ Describe the events of their rebellion
- ▶ Explain why the rebellion was a Scottish civil war

How did the Jacobites begin?

In 1688, the Dutch Prince William of Orange was invited to England. He was asked to kick out the **Catholic** King James VII of Scotland (and II of England). The government wanted to increase the power of parliament and unite both countries under one **Protestant** king.

James' main supporters in Scotland were led by Viscount 'Bonnie' Dundee. His army ambushed William's troops at dusk on 27 July 1689 as they marched through the narrow pass of Killiecrankie in Perthshire. Hundreds were killed. But victory was short-lived and James was eventually defeated by William at the Battle of the Boyne in 1690.

What next for supporters of the Stuarts?

After the death of Queen Anne in 1714, George of Hanover became king of Britain. He was a dull and unpopular German prince.

James Stuart, the son of James VII, had a better claim to be king, but he was Catholic and therefore not allowed. James became known as the **pretender** to the throne. His Catholic supporters in Britain were known as the followers of James or **Jacobites**. In the Highlands, many clan chiefs remained loyal to James and disobeyed the government by taking part in two rebellions in 1715 and 1745.

 Activate your brain cells!

- Choose three words to describe yourself now and three more to describe who you would like to be in a few years' time.
- If you feel comfortable, suggest three **positive** words to describe your partner.
- Why is it useful to know our own strengths and to find out what others think they are?

The '15

In 1715 the Earl of Mar gathered an army of 12,000 men in support of James. They were mostly southern highlanders and men who opposed the union of 1707. But before James could arrive from France, the government army, led by the Earl of Argyll, defeated the Jacobites at Sheriffmuir.

The '45

In 1745 James' son tried to get his father crowned king. Aged just 25, the '**Bonnie Prince**' Charles Edward Stuart sailed to Scotland and landed at Lochiel. His enthusiasm and charm persuaded many Highland chiefs to add their army to his. The Glenfinnan Monument marks the spot where Bonnie Prince Charlie raised the Stuart flag and started his rebellion.

But some clans, like the Campbells, supported the government. Other families stayed out of it. Many families fought brother against brother, father against son. Charles had caused a Scottish **civil war**.

A transcript from an interview with a Jacobite soldier in 1746

Interviewer: What happened after you joined Charles' army last year?

Jacobite soldier: We swept down through the Highlands to Edinburgh and captured it without a fight on 17 September 1745.

I: What happened next?

JS: We heard that the commander of the government troops, Sir John Cope, had landed an army at Dunbar so we marched to meet them. At dawn we surprised them at Prestonpans. We smashed them with our Highland charge and they fled!

I: A famous victory. What did Charles do next?

JS: He wanted us to march all the way down to London! I thought it was a crazy idea, but the vote was won by a majority of one so we had to go.

I: You got as far as Derby and turned back. Why?

JS: We were only 127 miles from London, but what would we do when we got there? We hadn't fought many government troops on the way down, where were they all? We were running out of supplies, enthusiasm and we missed our loved ones.

We turned back with the Duke of Cumberland hot on our tails.

I: You reached Inverness and the flat moor of Culloden. Can you tell us about the battle on 16 April 1746?

JS: We were starving and exhausted – we'd marched all night to surprise the 9000 government troops but they were waiting for us. The ground was boggy and we could not fight easily with our broadswords. Our Highland charge was cut down by their guns. The leadership of Charles was so poor that my clan was ready to rebel. He'd sacked Lord George Murray, who was the only good general he had. The butcher Cumberland had his men give us '**no quarter**' and ran us down. His troops shot the wounded and the prisoners. I was lucky enough to escape, hundreds were not. I don't know where Charles fled to.

I: You must despise the English for what they did.

JS: I heard few English voices at Culloden. There were more Scots on the government side than in the whole of our army. It was a civil war. I fought against Lowlanders, Campbells from the Highlands, German soldiers for hire and Irish troops. I don't hate the English. I hate war.

🧩 Show your understanding

1. In pairs, read out the interview then answer the following questions:
   a) How does the soldier describe the battle of Prestonpans?
   b) How popular was Charles' decision to march to London among his generals?
   c) Why did the Jacobite army turn back at Derby?
   d) What weaknesses did the Jacobite army have at Culloden? What consequence might each one have had in the battle?
   e) How did the Duke of Cumberland earn the nickname 'butcher'?

2. Choose three words that describe the strengths of Charles Edward Stuart and three that describe his weaknesses.
3. Complete either a) or b).
   a) Find out more about the Battle of Culloden and expand the interview. Record a professional version using a video recorder or a microphone.
   b) Find out about the costume of government and Jacobite soldiers. Draw a battle scene and label two of the soldiers with the correct equipment.

How do you explain the witches?

What are we exploring?

By the end of this section you should be able to:

▶ Explain what happened to women accused of witchcraft

▶ Describe some of the real reasons women were accused

▶ Imagine why societies believed in witches

Activate your brain cells!

- Have you ever been wrongly suspected of something? Share an example with a partner.
- Why do people 'jump to conclusions' about others?

Until the late seventeenth century, many Europeans believed in witches and witchcraft. They accused innocent people of working with the Devil to force people to become sinners and so go to hell.

Many people were put on trial for witchcraft in the sixteenth and seventeenth centuries. In some places, a witch-finder was employed to find witches and prove they were guilty.

All sorts of events, problems and tragedies were blamed on witchcraft. In Scotland, between 1563 and 1727 about 4000 people were accused of witchcraft. Many were publicly humiliated, tortured and killed by strangling or burning. Eighty-five per cent of them were women.

Source A – the trial of Margaret Harkett in 1585

The accused witch is a 60 year-old widow. She was caught picking peas in Joan Frynde's field without her permission. When Mrs Frynde asked her to give the peas back, she became angry and threw the peas to the ground. From that time on, no peas would grow in the field.
A neighbour bought a pair of shoes from Margaret, but he did not have enough money. He later fell from a pear tree and died from his injuries.

Source B – a witness in the case of Joan Flower and her daughters

Joan Flower looks like a witch and does not believe in God. Her daughter Margaret used to steal from Belvoir Castle, where she worked. When he found out, the Earl of Rutland threw her out. Soon after, the Earl and his wife became ill. Their eldest son Henry died and the other two children are still ill. Joan and her daughters have used witchcraft to punish the Earl and his family for the dismissal of Margaret. (Joan, Margaret and Philllipa were all found guilty and hanged.)

Source C

These animals were supposed to suck blood from a mark on the witch's body. Before a trial the accused woman was examined for any suspicious marks. If a mark was found on her body it was seen as proof that she was a witch. What might such marks have really been?

Source D

How to know whether a woman is a witch or not

Source E – written in 1631 by Frederich von Spee, who spoke out against the witch trials

If she does not confess, the torture is repeated – twice, thrice, four times. There is no limit. Now, under severe stress and pain she declares herself guilty. She also condemns others, of whom she knows no ill, whose names are suggested to her by the witch-finder. These 'witches' are then put on trial and also treated in the same way.

Historians have suggested several reasons why European societies treated people in this way.

Show your understanding

1. Write a brief definition for a sixteenth century dictionary explaining what the word **witch** means. Read sources A to E for information.
2. Find at least two different methods that were used to prove that people were witches. For each method, say why it was an unreliable method.
3. In pairs, design leaflets for either a) or b).
   a) Write as though you are a witch-hunter alerting people to the witches in your village. Include an explanation of why people should beware of suspicious women.
   b) Write as someone against witch-hunts, telling people why the trials are wrong. Include an explanation of why women in particular are the victims of witch-hunts.

The old single woman used to be valued and respected by her community. Neighbours might have once asked her to heal people using herbs and basic medical knowledge. However, in times of anxiety, the woman who was once the 'wise' woman of the village became the witch. People became worried about her special and strange powers.

There may have been some poor and powerless women who believed in witchcraft. They probably did curse people. This may have been the only way they could have got their own back on a society where they had no help or hope of help.

*People looked for witches to blame for their problems. They were used as **scapegoats**. Single, elderly women were more likely to be beggars than men, because men had more chance of getting work. It tended to be these poor, old widows who were accused most often.*

48 How did Scots invent the modern world?

What are we exploring?

By the end of this section you should be able to:

▶ Explain what the Scottish Enlightenment was

▶ Describe some of the key people and their discoveries

▶ Imagine how important these discoveries have become today

In the eighteenth century, belief in witches, demons and evil spirits was defeated forever by **thinking.** Thinkers across Europe made attempts to build on their knowledge. Their goal was to help mankind. The time of this search for knowledge is known as the **Age of Reason** or the **Enlightenment**.

These thinkers did not want to believe in myths and mystery. The dark 'unknown' was only that which they had not yet understood or shed light on. Some of the most important **enlightened** thinkers between 1750 and 1800 came from Scotland.

What did they think about?

They explored ideas about God, curiosity about life and death, science, economies, religions. They made the first real study of why people and society have changed.

Who were these people?

Adam Smith had perhaps the biggest impact on Britain. His ideas about money and the economy have influenced politicians to this day.

- Henry Raeburn – painting
- David Hume – philosophy
- James Hutton – geology
- Robert Adam – architecture
- Alexander Monro – medicine
- John Gregory – mathematics
- Joseph Black – chemistry

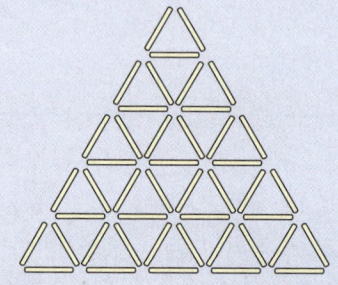

Activate your brain cells!

- Take your time over this puzzle. How many triangles are there in this picture?

- Why might having more time to think things through give you better results?
- How much time a day do you spend just thinking?

Where?

The Enlightenment occurred in the Scottish cities. Edinburgh was the main city for the Enlightenment, although Glasgow and Aberdeen had forward-thinkers too.

Edinburgh's New Town was cosy enough for its **intelligentsia** to be able to meet regularly in clubs and societies. One excited visitor wrote 'Here I stand, at what is called the Cross of Edinburgh and within a few minutes take 50 men of genius by the hand.'

Why now?

> The Union of 1707 created peace and wealth in Scotland. Close connections with London allowed the Enlightenment thinkers to build on the knowledge of the English. Put simply, the Scots had time to think.
>
> Historian A

> The Scottish church, law courts, schools and universities were not affected by the 1707 Union. So the ideas and strong education of Scots before the Union were allowed to continue. Nearly all Scots thinkers all went to their local school and all went to one of the Scottish universities.
>
> Historian B

Show your understanding

1. Write a sentence or two to explain why Scotland should be proud of its Enlightenment heritage.
2. Complete this table using the speech bubbles from Historian A and Historian B.

Evidence that the Enlightenment was due to the Union of 1707	Evidence that the Enlightenment would have happened anyway

3. Who are important thinkers in Scotland today? Who could be the important thinkers in a future Scotland?
4. Find out more about one of the Scottish Enlightenment thinkers. Choose one who studied a subject you like. Present your fact file as a leaflet, a pretend interview or a podcast lesson for the rest of the class.

Titanic timeline team treasure hunt!

This challenge involves your team reviewing all the topics in this book and checking your understanding of the connections between the topics. Match up all the dates with the correct events and put them in chronological order. Look back over the book to help you.

13000BC	7000BC	5000BC	4000BC	3500BC	3000BC	2611BC
1184BC	600BC	550BC	490BC	480BC	AD43	AD84
AD122	AD142	AD306	AD367	AD397	AD410	AD411
AD476	AD563	AD610	AD793	AD843	AD911	AD1066
AD1072	AD1085	AD1215	AD1096–99	AD1147–49	AD1189–92	AD1202–04
AD1262	AD1286	AD1292	AD1296	AD1297	AD1298	AD1305
AD1306	AD1314	AD1320	AD1347	AD1450	AD1492	AD1517
AD1519	AD1560	AD1566	Feb AD1567	Mar AD1567	Aug AD1567	AD1587
AD1620	AD1642	AD1645	AD1660	AD1689	AD1707	AD1745
AD1746						

o Lord Darnley is murdered at Kirk O Field.

o Legend has it that the Myceneans attacked and captured Troy.

o 15,000 years ago the land we now call Scotland was covered in a sheet of ice hundreds of meters thick.

o 16 April, Jacobites lose at the Battle of Culloden.

o A political Union between Scotland and England is signed.

o A ship returns from Africa to Europe with the plague on board.

o Alexander III of Scotland is killed.

o Ancient Egyptian civilisation begins on the Nile.

o Approximate date of the invention of the printing press.

o Athens and Sparta beat the Persians at the battle of Marathon.

o August. Mary flees Scotland hoping Elizabeth I will help her.

o Columbus sets foot on the West Indies and becomes the first European to set foot in Americas since the Vikings.

o Confucius is said to have developed his philosphy Confucianism.

o Cortes marches through Mexico to capture it for the Spanish.

o Emperor Antoninus orders the Antonine wall to be built.

o Emperor Constantine becomes the first Christian emperor.

o Emperor Hadrian orders the building of a wall to divide Northern Britain from the south.

o First settlers in Ancient China live along the Yangtze River.

o German Goths capture Rome – the Roman Empire in the West is finished. The Eastern Byzantine empire continues from Constantinople.

o Jacobites win at Prestonpans and get as far south as Derby before returning to Scotland.

- John Balliol made King of Scotland at Scone.
- Kenneth MacAlpin unites three kingdoms into one and calls it Alba. The idea of Scotland is born.
- King Charles declares war on his parliament – the British Civil war begins.
- Lao Tzu is believed to have begun the philosophy of Taoism.
- Lindisfarne attacked by Viking raiders.
- Magna Carta signed at Runnymede limiting the King's power.
- March. Mary marries Bothwell.
- Marco Polo sets off along the Silk road to explore the Far East.
- Martin Luther is expelled from the Catholic Church for criticising it as corrupt. He starts the Reformation of the church to Protestantism.
- Mary beheaded at Fotheringay Castle on the orders of Elizabeth I.
- Mary Queen of Scots arrives in Leith from France.
- Mesopotamian civilisation begins between the Tigris and Euphrates rivers in modern-day Iraq.
- Mohammed begins teaching the Muslim faith.
- 11 November, the Pilgrim Fathers arrive in Plymouth.
- Picts smash through Hadrian's Wall.
- Rizzio is murdered by Lord Darnley.
- Robert the Bruce kills John Comyn at Greyfriars Kirk.
- Roman army invades Britain under leadership of General Agricola.
- Roman troops leave Britain.
- Rome invaded by the Visigoth tribes.
- Skara Brae settlement.

- Sparta lose to the Persians at the Battle of Thermoplyae.
- St Columba establishes the monastry and church of Iona.
- St. Ninian becomes a bishop and sets up the first Scottish church in Whithorn.
- The Battle of Bannockburn.
- The Battle of Falkirk.
- The Battle of Stirling Bridge.
- The Declaration of Arbroath is signed and sent off to the Pope.
- The Domesday book is ordered to collect information about William's new lands.
- The First Crusade.
- The first people appeared in Scotland.
- The first Pyramid built by Ihohtep for the Pharoh Djoser.
- The fourth Crusade.
- The Jacobites, led by Bonnie Dundee, win at Killiecrankie.
- The Normans invade Britain and defeat King Harold at the Battle of Hastings.
- The Restoration of the Monarchy – Charles II is made King.
- The Romans defeat Calgacus' Caledonians at Mons Graupius.
- The Royalists are defeated by Cromwell's Parliamentarians at the Battle of Naseby.
- The sack of Berwick upon Tweed and the battle of Dunbar.
- The second Crusade.
- The third Crusade.
- The Viking prince Rollo invades northern France and sets up the Norman kingdom.
- William the Conquerer takes control of Scotland without much opposition.
- William Wallace is executed in London in August.

Put the dates and events on a timeline and divide them up into Scottish, British, European and World events. Make your timeline big. The bigger the better! Use all the wall and floor space your teacher will let you use.

When did Google begin?

What are we exploring?

By the end of this section you should be able to:

▶ Explain a little bit about what Google is and does
▶ Understand that Google has evolved quickly
▶ Describe how an Internet search actually works

⚙ **Activate your brain cells!**

- Do you remember life before Google? Can you name any other Internet search engines? Discuss this with the person next to you.
- As well as web searches, can you name any other services that Google offers? See if you can get more on your list than your partner.

What is Google?

Google Inc. is an American company specialising in Internet searching. It **generates** 99 per cent of its profits from adverts that are similar and targeted to the search terms that you type in. Google makes about $4 million a day from online advertising – it's no wonder that everyone who works for Google gets free meals in the company café!

Since Google was formed in 1996 it has been one of the fastest growing companies in the world and its homepage has become the most visited website on the Internet. Due to its massive growth, it has also expanded into other areas such as online video, digitised books and software.

Google's company mission statement is 'to organise the world's information and make it universally accessible and useful'. Its unofficial slogan is 'don't be evil'.

Some important bits of Google history

Larry Page and Sergey Brin

- Google began in March 1996 as a research project by Larry Page and Sergey Brin, who were PhD students at Stanford University, California.

- The **domain name** google.com was registered on 14 September 1997 and the Google Corporation was formed a year later in September 1998.

- Google started selling adverts with its keyword searches in 2000. Their adverts programs 'AdWords' and 'AdSense' were created and the company finally had a source of income other than **venture capital** from private investors.

- Google moved its offices to a large estate (nicknamed the GooglePlex) in Mountainview, California, in 2003, and it is still based there today. It also has lots of other offices around the world.

The GooglePlex

A Google Streetview car

- In 2004, Google launched Google Earth.
- In 2006, the verb 'to Google' was officially added to the Oxford English Dictionary. Google also bought YouTube for $1.65 billion!
- Google's Android mobile development platform was launched in 2007.
- Steetview, a controversial new Google project, came to the UK in 2008.
- 2009 saw the introduction of Google Wave and also the announcement of the Google Chrome operating system.

How much data does Google generate?

Google runs thousands of servers across the world. Between them they process millions of search requests every day and about one **petabyte** of user-generated data each hour.

What is a petabyte?

Well, you will have heard of megabytes and gigabytes before (1000 megabytes = 1 gigabyte). You might have also heard of terabytes (1000 gigabytes = 1 terabyte). A petabyte is 1000 terabytes – a lot of data!

 Show your understanding

1. What do you think is meant by the term 'venture capital'? (Clue: remember the word adventure often involves risk!)
2. How do you think Google is faring in achieving its mission statement? Does everyone have access to its search technology?
3. Why do you think Goggle's unofficial slogan is 'don't be evil'? What do you think this actually means?
4. Write down the three things that you think have been the most important in the company's development and why.
5. Design a Google homepage logo for your birthday or other important event of your choosing.

Explore further

6. Find out what a PhD is.
7. Work out how much money Google makes in a whole year from adverts.
8. Deciding on your own scale, plot 1 megabite, 1 gigabite, 1 terabite and 1 petabyte on a graph – a logarithmic graph might help you here.

Bore your friends...

The Google phrase 'PageRank' is actually named after Google founder Larry Page and not the order in which things appear on the screen.

50 Who answered questions before Google?

What are we exploring?

By the end of this section you should be able to:

▶ Describe a number of different places from which you can get information

▶ Explain the differences between primary and secondary sources

▶ Understand the things to look for in a reliable website

Over two billion searches are done using Google each day. But where did we get our information from before Google? Also, how do we even know that Google is right?

Libraries: for years, libraries were one of our main sources of information. Interestingly, thousands of old library books have been scanned into Google and are now fully searchable. Lots of library books are now out of date.

Other people: we gain a lot of information from people that we trust or we think are an expert in the subject (e.g. parents, politicians and teachers).

Media: television, radio and newspapers all contribute to giving us knowledge over time. However, any media source may be biased and unreliable – that's why newspapers and TV companies often have to give apologies.

Finding things out for ourselves: human beings have always been naturally **inquisitive**, particularly at a local level. It's more difficult to actually experience things if you live a long way away from them. The Internet can help us feel closer to events around the world. Many people now share their personal experiences on their own websites (Facebook, MySpace and other blogs).

Activate your brain cells!

- Have you ever found a website that is completely inaccurate? How did you know?
- Share your experience with your class.

Types of sources

All of the sources of information here can be described as either primary or secondary. We learned about this in section 4.

How do I know if a website is reliable?

Check the **extension** on the web address. If it ends in .gov (government), .edu (educational institution) or .mil (military), then the information has been **vetted** (checked) before it was put online. Website addresses with .gov, .edu and .mil have to be applied for, and their use is controlled. But websites with .org, .net, .com and .co.uk can be purchasd by anyone.

Look for an **author**. If someone has put their name on the page, it it is more likely to be reliable. Research the author, see if there is any information that helps you to judge their reliability. If the author can't be contacted or has no expertise in the subject they have written about, the website may be questionable.

See if the website is part of a **larger site**. It might not make a big difference, but if the website is linked to an organisation that has a trustworthy reputation, the chances are that the website is also more reliable.

Try to find a 'last updated' **date**. If the date is some time ago, it may be the case that the website was once reliable but is now out of date.

Consider whether it has been **professionally produced** or designed.

That alone does not help to prove that the site is reliable, but it can help to prove that it is hosted and written by a professional.

The growth of Google searches

1998: 10,000 searches a day

1999: 3 million searches a day

2000: 18 million searches a day

2002: 150 million searches a day

2004: 200 million searches a day

2007: 1.2 billion searches a day

2008: 2 billion searches a day

Show your understanding

1. Make your own version of the table below and fill it in.

	Libraries	Television	Asking people	Investigation
Advantages				
Disadvantages				

2. In your own words, describe the difference between a primary and a secondary source.

3. The following things are all types of sources. Put them into a diagram like the one shown below. If you think any of the things could be both, put them in the middle.

- mobile phone photograph
- book about the 1800s
- YouTube video on the Romans
- Second World War diary
- live podcast
- an old Polaroid
- someone telling you they 'saw it with their own eyes'
- a blog from the 2008 Chinese earthquake
- unedited CCTV or webcam footage
- a webpage

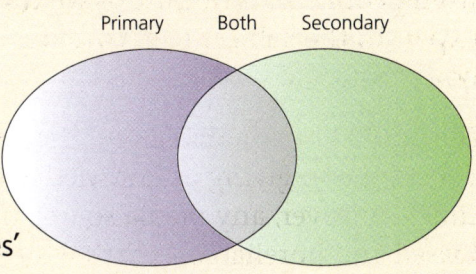

4. How can the Internet improve our access to primary sources? (Re-read section 4 if you can't remember the definition of a primary source.)

5. Turn the information on website reliability into 5–10 easy-to-remember bullet points. Make this into a poster, leaflet or something else (be creative!).

6. Plot the information about Google's growth on a graph and describe it using at least three sentences.

How can using Google make me a better learner?

By the end of this section you should be able to:

▶ Understand how to use the Google advanced search
▶ Think about how you might use some of the other Google search tools

Being able to search the Internet well is an important skill. Unfortunately, it's also something that we don't tend to be very good at. Most people just type one or two words into Google or another search engine and press 'search' or 'find'. People normally then go to the first webpage on the list. While this is appropriate some of the time, it's not particularly accurate and its certainly not 'smart searching'.

 Activate your brain cells!

- Think back to primary school. When were you first taught to search the Internet? Was it a good lesson?
- Imagine you want to find out some information about your local area. What would be the best three words to type into a search?

Smarter searching

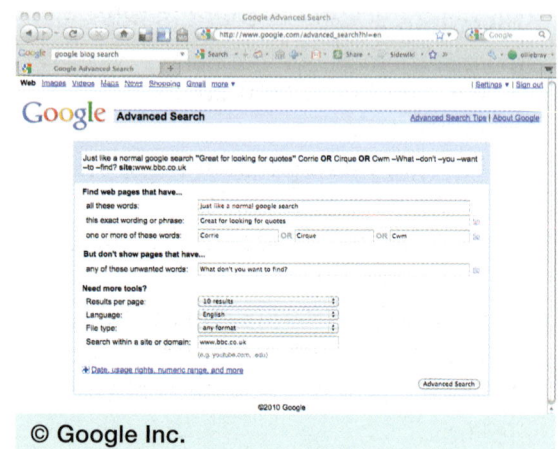

© Google Inc.

One of the smartest ways to search Google is to try the 'Advanced Search' function. An advanced search allows you to really narrow down your search options so that you can find exactly what you're looking for.

Other Google search options

As well as a standard web search, Google also offers a number of other search tools that are particularly useful in social subjects. These are:

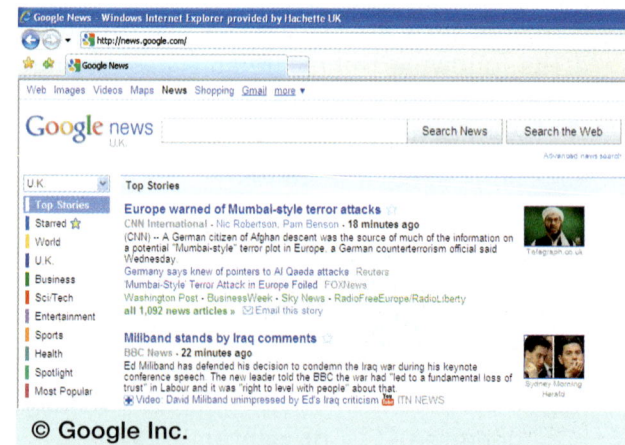

© Google Inc.

Google News (news.google.com) is a computer-generated news site that **aggregates** (gathers) headlines from more than 4,500 approved news sources worldwide and groups any similar stories together.

Not only can you get up-to-date news, but you can also search historical news archives. Some newspapers have been digitised and go as far back as the 1500s. I bet you never thought you would see a book that old!

© Google Inc.

Google Blog™ Search (blogsearch. google.com) Blogs are self-published websites written by normal people (although lots of big companies have blogs as well).

Blogs can give eyewitness accounts and photographs from when events actually happen. They can be a great source of information to give a personal perspective on local, national and international events.

© Google Inc.

Google Books™ Search Service (books. google.com) searches thousands of books that have been scanned in and digitised from all over the world. Some of the books are now out of copyright, so you can read the complete work online. In other cases only extracts of the book are available but, using the search tool, you can find out where you can buy or borrow a copy of the full text.

Books are fantastic secondary sources of information, and as they are digitised they are really easy to search. Some Google digitised books are hundreds of years old!

 Show your understanding

1. Type the word 'history' into the search engines of Google, Yahoo and Bing. Compare the top ten results from each. Are they the same, similar or very different?
2. Have a look at www.quintura.com. It's a visual search engine. How do you think visual searching could help you with your learning?
3. Using Google News Search:
   a) What is the earliest newspaper article about Scotland that you can find?
   b) What is 'hot' in the news today?
   c) What was the most important news event on the day you were born? (You being born doesn't count!)
4. Can you work out how to create your own personalised online newspaper using Google News Search? (Note: you will need a Google account for this.)
5. Using Google Blog Search:
   a) Can you find a blog about volcanoes?
   b) Can you find a blog on the most recent Winter Olympics?
   c) Can you find a blog on the place where you live?
6. Describe to your partner what makes a good blog (for example presentation, quality of the writing, length of the posts etc.)
7. Using Google Book Search:
   a) Can you find your favourite book as a child?
   b) Can you find the last book that you read?
   c) Can you find a book that you would like to read next?
8. Check out Google Scholar. What do you think this is used for? Why is its tag line 'Stand on the shoulders of giants'?

Why is Google a global business?

What are we exploring?

By the end of this section you should be able to:

▶ Describe Google's presence around the world

▶ Explain what a multinational company is

▶ Understand a little bit more about diversity and web censorship

How has Google grown?

Before 1996 no one had ever heard of Google. Since that time it has expanded from its two founders (Larry and Sergey) to employ nearly 20,000 people all over the world. Google is one the fastest-growing companies in history.

Where is Google around the world?

Google is an example of a **multinational** company because it employs people in lots of different places. It has offices in over 40 countries. This map below shows their main locations.

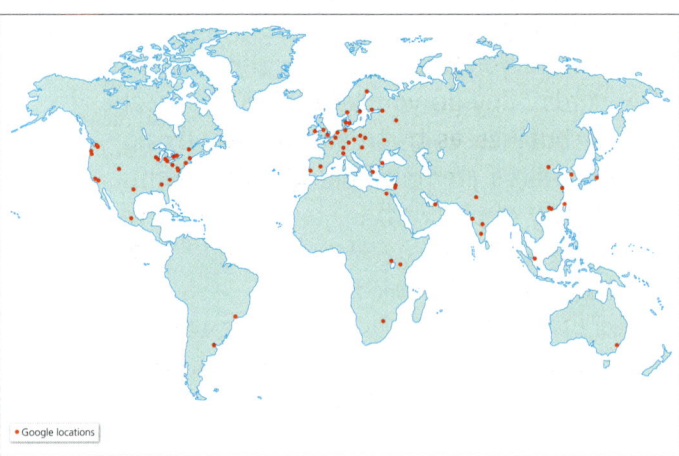

Google locations

Activate your brain cells!

- Can you think of a good name for a search engine? Why do you think it's good? Discuss this with your partner; decide whose name is best and why.
- Discuss with a partner why you think Google has been able to grow so quickly.

Google offices in the US and London.

Celebrating diversity and multiculturalism

A diverse workforce.

Multiculturalism is the acceptance or promotion of multiple ethnic cultures.

Multicultural companies advocate equal rights to all employees without promoting any specific ethnic, religious or cultural values as company policy. Many countries such as the USA and UK have laws that promote equal opportunities and non-discrimination during employment and recruitment. In the UK, the main laws to protect employees are all grouped within the Equality Act.

Google is a multicultural and diverse company, not just because of its range of products but also because of the range of people that it employs. After all, over 50 per cent of people who use Google do not speak English as their first language.

In May 2007, Google started its '40 Languages Initiative'. The aim was to get Google products into 40 languages, mapping to roughly 70 countries. This initiative would allow 99.3 per cent of the Internet population to have access to Google's products.

Diversity and inclusion are fundamental to Google's way of doing things. We strive to be a local company in every country in which we operate, and we understand that our users have different cultures, languages, and traditions. It drives the projects we work on, the people we hire, and the goals we set ourselves. We go to great lengths to create products that are useful to our users wherever they are, and we've found that this commitment to diversity and to our users has been key to our success.

Nikesh Arora, President, EMEA Operations

 Show your understanding

1. Give five key points about the location of Google's offices around the world.
2. Look at the picture of people working for Google. What evidence is there to suggest this is a fun working environment? Why do you think Google like their employees to have fun?
3. Imagine you wanted to apply for a job at Google. Decide the type of job and then write down ten things about you that would secure you your chosen job. What skills make you stand out from other applicants?
4. Describe multiculturalism in your own words. Why do you think it is important for businesses to be multicultural?
5. As well as promoting multiculturalism, what other reasons might Google have for translating their products into over 40 different languages?
6. Look at Nikesh Arora's quote – why do you think she places such an emphasis on 'local' and 'community'?

How environmentally friendly is Google?

What are we exploring?

By the end of this section you should be able to:

▶ Understand the true cost of Internet searching

▶ Explain renewable energy and describe some of the ways that Google is using it

Google needs a lot of computers to run its service. These are grouped together to form **servers** and are stored in large data centres around the world. It is estimated that Google maintains over 500,000 servers worldwide.

Activate your brain cells!

- List five things that you could do to be more environmentally friendly.
- Now list the five reasons that you are not currently doing these things.

How much does it cost to do a web search?

You might think that searching the Internet is free, but there are a number of hidden costs. First of all your computer or phone needs power (your parents will probably be paying for this). Plus, every time you search the Internet it needs to use a data centre and these data centres use a lot of electricity.

Google says that one quick search produces about 0.2g of CO_2. But scientists at Harvard University estimate that, because we are not very good at online searching, by the time we have found what we are looking for we will have created about 7g of CO_2. This means that two detailed searches are about the equivalent of boiling a kettle.

Environmentally friendly data centres

In the past Google has received negative publicity about the amount of electricity it uses in its data centres. However, it has

come up with some **innovative** solutions for making better use of, and investing in, **renewable energy**.

Renewable energy makes use of natural resources that are unlikely to run out or can be replaced if used in a sustainable way.

Hydroelectricity

In Dallas, Google built a data centre that uses cheap hydroelectricity from the Columbia River.

Wind farms

The Netherlands is very flat and quite windy; it has long been famous for windmills. When Google set up their data centre here they decided to use wind power to provide some of the electricity. They also plan to build a wind farm to provide at least 18 per cent of the power to their data centre in Iowa, USA.

Wave power

In 2007, Google filed a patent application for a wave-powered server farm. The idea is simple: the servers are kept on a huge boat

and the power for them comes from a massive network of wave buoys surrounding it. Sea water would also be used as the cooling system to stop the whole operation from overheating.

Solar power

In 2007, Google installed over 9,000 solar panels on the rooftops of eight buildings and two carports at their GooglePlex headquarters in California.

This installation produces enough electricity to power about 30 per cent of Google's peak electricity demand. That's the equivalent of approximately 1,200 Scottish houses.

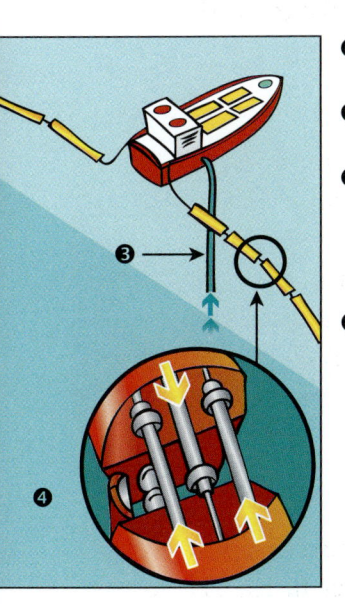

❶ Databarges will be moored about 3–7 miles off the coast.

❷ Electricity is generated by wave power.

❸ Electricity will power the ship and computers. Pumps will suck up cold sea water and circulate it around computers to keep them cool.

❹ As the sections move against each other, hydraulic rams resist the movement. The power produced is used to drive generators.

Show your understanding

1. Explain how getting better at web searching can help the environment.
2. In your own words, explain what is meant by renewable energy.
3. For **either** hydroelectricity or wind power, prepare a 30-second radio news bulletin explaining Google's projects in Dallas or The Netherlands.
4. Look at Google's plans for a wave-powered data centre.
   a) Do you think this idea will actually work? Write down the reasons for your thinking.
   b) What problems might occur when you keep computer equipment on a boat at sea?
5. Design your own way to power a data centre using renewable energy. Present your idea as a labelled diagram.
6. If Google contribute one per cent of their annual profits to Google.org every year, how much is that in US dollars? (Chapter 49 might help you with this.)

Explore further

Check out google.com/corporate/solarpanels/home. You can actually see how much energy the GooglePlex is generating. Why do you think it doesn't generate much in the morning?

How is Google helping developing countries?

What are we exploring?

By the end of this section you should be able to:

▶ Give examples of how Google has helped less developing countries

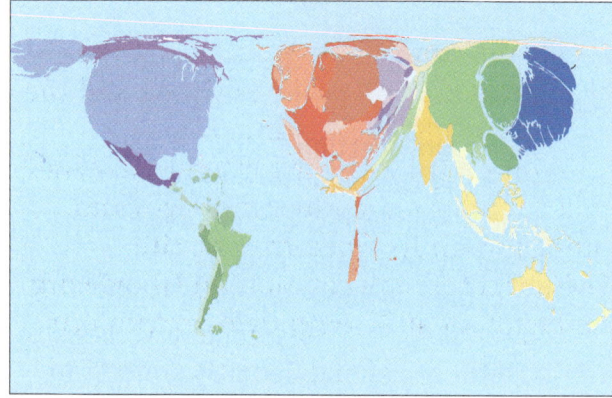

Activate your brain cells!

- This map shows global Internet users – why do you think it doesn't look like a normal world map?

What has Google done to help developing countries?

Google.org, the charitable arm of Google, has provided a lot of support to developing countries including:

Guinea worm in Ghana

Guinea worm is a **parasite** that can live and grow inside the human body and is contracted by drinking **contaminated** water. **Extraction** of the worm is a painful process which involves wrapping it around a stick and slowly pulling it out. In some cases this can take as long as a month.

Google.org provided $1,450,000 to match funding from the Carter Centre to support Guinea worm **eradication** in Ghana.

Tackling deforestation

Deforestation is the clearance of naturally occurring forests by humans by logging and burning trees. Deforestation can lead to soil erosion and also the destruction of important global **ecosystems**. It is a particular problem in developing countries and, although lots of people in developed countries have heard of deforestation, they remain unaware of the real scale of the problem.

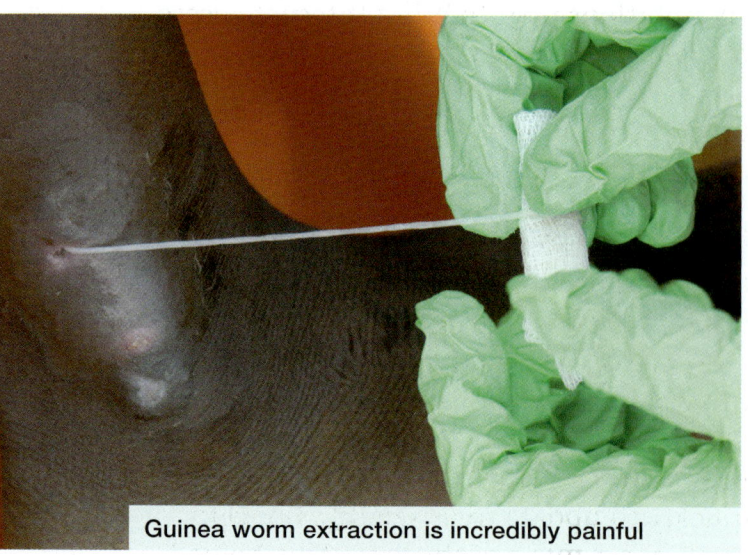
Guinea worm extraction is incredibly painful

Tracking deforestation in Google Earth

Google.org has provided a $2 million multi-year grant to support the satellite mapping of forests in tropical countries. This makes use of the company's Google Map and Google Earth software. Its aim is not only to gather data on the true scale of deforestation but also to improve awareness of the problem.

Improving connectivity in Africa

We are very lucky to have good Internet speeds across most of the UK but some parts of the world have very poor access. **Connectivity** is particularly poor in most parts of rural Africa. But a good Internet connection and access to associated technology can provide rural communities with a way to communicate with the outside world, access to education and valuable health information.

In 2008 Google provided some funding for an ambitious plan to bring Internet access to over three billion people in Africa by launching sixteen satellites that have the capacity to provide fast broadband to some of the world's most remote areas.

Disaster relief

Google.org also donates the time and services of Google employees to give short-term aid after natural disasters. For example, after Hurricane Katrina destroyed much of downtown New Orleans in the USA in 2005, Google engineers worked quickly to update their satellite imagery and impact maps of the area. This helped raise awareness of the scale of the disaster and assisted rescue workers in assessing the damage and organising the rescue effort.

Google did similar things following the 2008 Sichuan Earthquake in China and the 2009 Hurricane Ketsana that hit the Philippines. It also allows international aid agencies to promote their messages and campaigns on its video-sharing site YouTube. More information on Google.org can be found at: www.google.org/projects.

 Show your understanding

1. Make a list of advantages and disadvantages that the Internet may bring to developing countries.
2. a) Why do you think Google.org was created?
   b) Use the Internet to find out the aims of Google.org (you might like to do this task at home).
3. Apart from it being a helpful thing to do, why else might Google be interested in improving Internet access in Africa?
4. Can you think of any other Internet technology that could be useful to developing countries?
5. Pick **either** the Guinea worm or deforestation. Research the topic in detail and agree with your teacher on how you will present your findings.

🔍 Explore further

Find out what Google did after Hurricane Katrina at earth.google.com/Katrina.

55 How do I explore history with Google Earth?

What are we exploring?

By the end of this section you should be able to:

▶ Explain why satellite images and aerial photographs are useful

▶ Navigate around Google Earth more confidently

▶ Use the historical imagery and other layers within Google Earth

What is Google Earth?

Google Earth lets you go anywhere on Earth to view satellite imagery, maps, **terrain** and 3D buildings. You can fly from the galaxies of outer space to the canyons and ocean trenches of our world. It helps you explore geographical and historical imagery and add layers of information about people and society. You can even save details of all of the places you have toured and share them with your friends.

Satellites and aerial photography

Arthur's Seat, Edinburgh, from above

An aerial photograph is a picture taken from the air. Aerial photographs used to be taken from planes and, before that, hot air balloons! Now most aerial photographs are taken by powerful satellites orbiting the Earth.

 Activate your brain cells!

- Have you used Google Earth before?
- Share some of the places that you have explored with the rest of your class. Your teacher will lead the discussion.
- If everywhere in the world has been photographed from above, how does this affect your privacy rights?

Satellite and aerial photography are really useful for exploring and discovering a place. You can also compare old and new images to see how an area has developed or changed with time.

Google Earth makes use of thousands (probably millions) of satellite images by splicing them all together into a 3D globe.

Google Earth

Site in 2001

Site in 2010

Historical imagery in Google Earth

You can turn on the historical imagery layer by clicking on the button along the top of the Google Earth menu.

The Beijing Olympic Stadium is a good example.

Great layers for discovering the past

As well as historical imagery, Google Earth has a layers menu that can help you find out more about the past. Lots of the layers will be interesting and useful in social subjects, but these ones are particularly valuable:

- **Rumseys Historical Maps** (global awareness layer): old maps from between 1680 and 1930. Great for learning about what places looked like in the past.
- **Global Heritage Fund** (global awareness layer): find out about ancient civilisations and how they are now being protected.
- **USHMM: Crisis in Darfur** (global awareness layer): find out what's happening in Darfur.
- **National Geographic** (global awareness layer): read reports and watch videos of historical, geographical and social journalism from around the world.
- **Volcanoes and Earthquakes** (gallery layer): find out about present and past volcanic eruptions and seismic earthquakes.

 Show your understanding

1. How might satellite images be useful for different people? Present your answer as a memory map.
2. Use Google Earth's controls to explore the following places:
   a) your house (just type in your postcode)
   b) your school
   c) Niagara Falls
   d) the Egyptian Pyramids
   e) Tower Bridge in London
   f) Sydney Opera House
   g) Mount Everest
   h) a place of your choosing (maybe where you went on holiday)
3. Can you work out how to look at the historical imagery of the Bird's Nest Olympic Stadium? What do you notice about how it developed over time?
4. Think about something that has been built recently near you. Spend some time exploring it with Google Earth.
5. Have a look at all of the different layers that are available in Google Earth. What is your favourite layer and which layers will be the most useful in school?

Explore further

You can download Google Earth for free on your computer at home. Just go to earth.google.com. Lots more information on using Google Earth can be found at: earth.google.com/userguide/v5.

Bore your friends...

Morocco's main Internet provider has been blocking Google Earth since August 2006 for undisclosed reasons.

How can Google help me learn about ancient Rome?

What are we exploring?

By the end of this section you should be able to:

▶ Share information about ancient Rome

▶ Understand why ancient Rome has been recreated in Google Earth

▶ Talk about your experience of exploring ancient Rome in Google Earth

Ancient Rome

Rome is the capital city of modern Italy and over 2,000 years ago it was the centre of the Roman Empire, one of the largest empires of its time. Legend has it that building the city started in 753BC, although historians and archaeologists agree that people were living in Rome long before this date.

Romulus and Remus

The legend of how Rome began

Twins Romulus and Remus were the sons of Mars (the Roman god of war). When they were babies, an evil uncle took them from their mother and threw them into the River Tiber to drown. Luckily, the babies floated to land and a mother wolf fed and cared for them. Later a herdsman looked after both boys until they grew up.

Many years later, Mars told his twin sons to build a city where they had been found. The city became Rome. One day, Remus made fun of the wall Romulus had built around the city. The twins argued, fought and Romulus ended up killing Remus.

Roman technology

Roman engineering was the most advanced of its time and they achieved some impressive technological feats. In fact, some of the engineering knowledge from the Romans was lost in the Middle Ages and not rediscovered until the nineteenth and twentieth centuries.

Construction during the Roman Empire included hundreds of roads, bridges, aqueducts, baths, theatres, arches and arenas.

Ancient Rome would have looked very different to modern Rome, although many monuments, such as the Coliseum, Pont du Gard and Pantheon, still remain as testaments to Roman engineering and the culture of the time.

Between 1933 and 1974, archaeologists created a model of what they believed the city would have looked like in AD320. The model city is housed in a special gallery in Rome's Museum of Roman Civilisation. In 2008, working with the museum, Google recreated Ancient Rome as a 3D layer in Google Earth.

Why recreate ancient Rome in Google Earth?

There are lots of reasons to recreate Rome in this way. Before Google added the ancient Rome layer to Google Earth, you would have actually had to visit the museum to be able to see how Rome would have looked originally. But now all you need is a computer and a free download. With this you can:

- view a virtual representation of the city in AD320, at the height of its development as the capital of the Roman Empire
- explore more than 6700 historic buildings
- zoom in to discover the detailed interiors of a number of ancient structures including the Coliseum
- learn about ancient Rome through information bubbles written by expert historians.

The Coliseum in Google Earth (© Google Inc.)

Rome's Coliseum (© Jen Deyenberg)

The Italian tourist board think that by recreating Rome in Google Earth more people will be inspired to visit the city.

 Show your understanding

In Google Earth, make sure that you have the 3D Building layer turned on and also the Ancient Rome 3D layer in the gallery menu.

1. Fly to Rome (type 'Ancient Rome' into the search box).
2. Explore the following locations and make brief notes about each place:
   a) the Coliseum
   b) Vatican City
   c) Tiber Island
   d) the Circus Maximus
   e) the Temple of Venus and Roma.
3. Pick your favourite place from the above list and go back to have a closer look.
   a) Use your Internet search skills to find out as much as possible about this place.
   b) Produce a script to attract tourists to this landmark. You can choose to present the script in any of the following formats: podcast, video, play, tourist leaflet, website or a mobile phone application.

Explore further

Lots more information about Rome is available at: earth.google.com/rome.

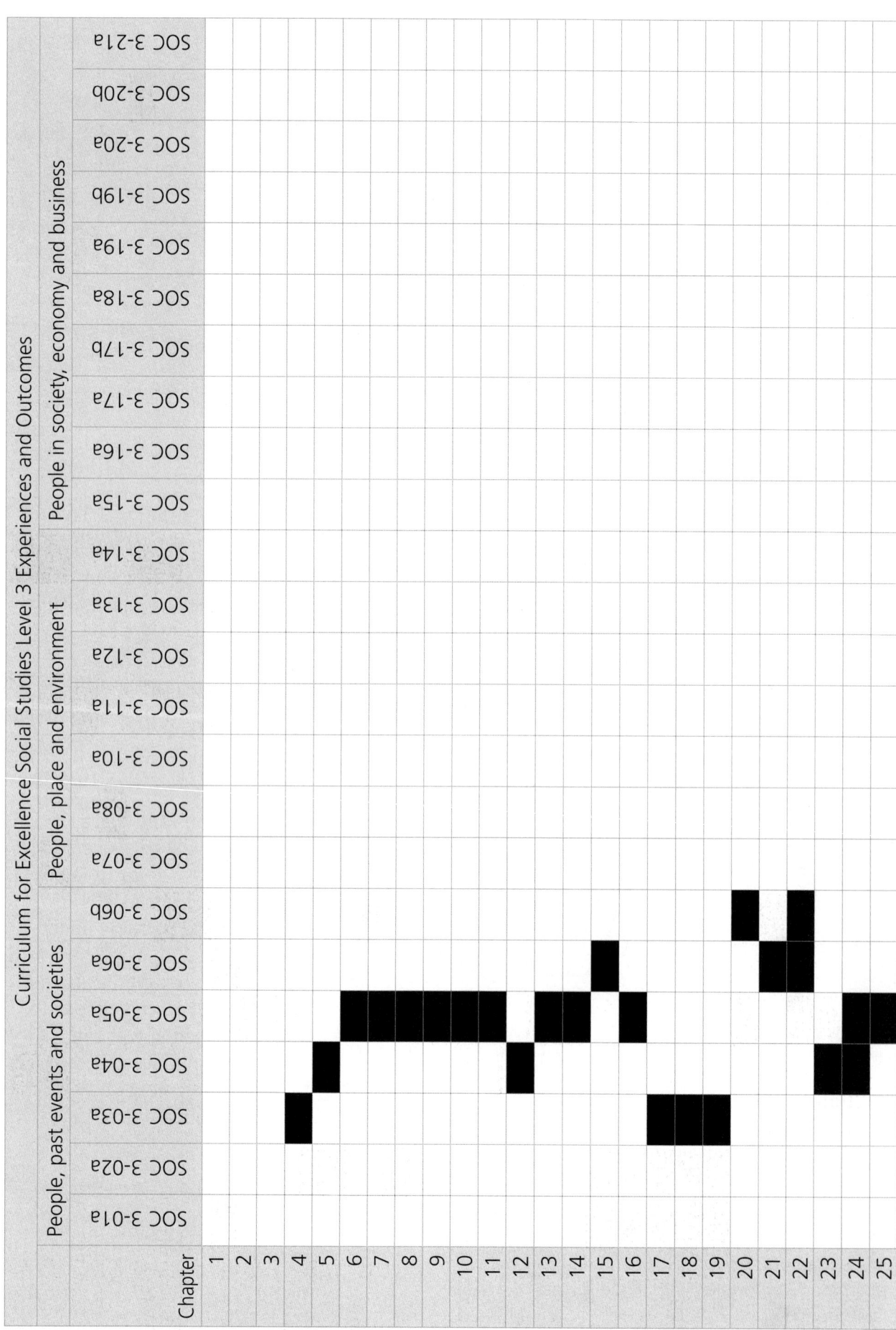

Curriculum for Excellence Social Studies Level 3 Experiences and Outcomes

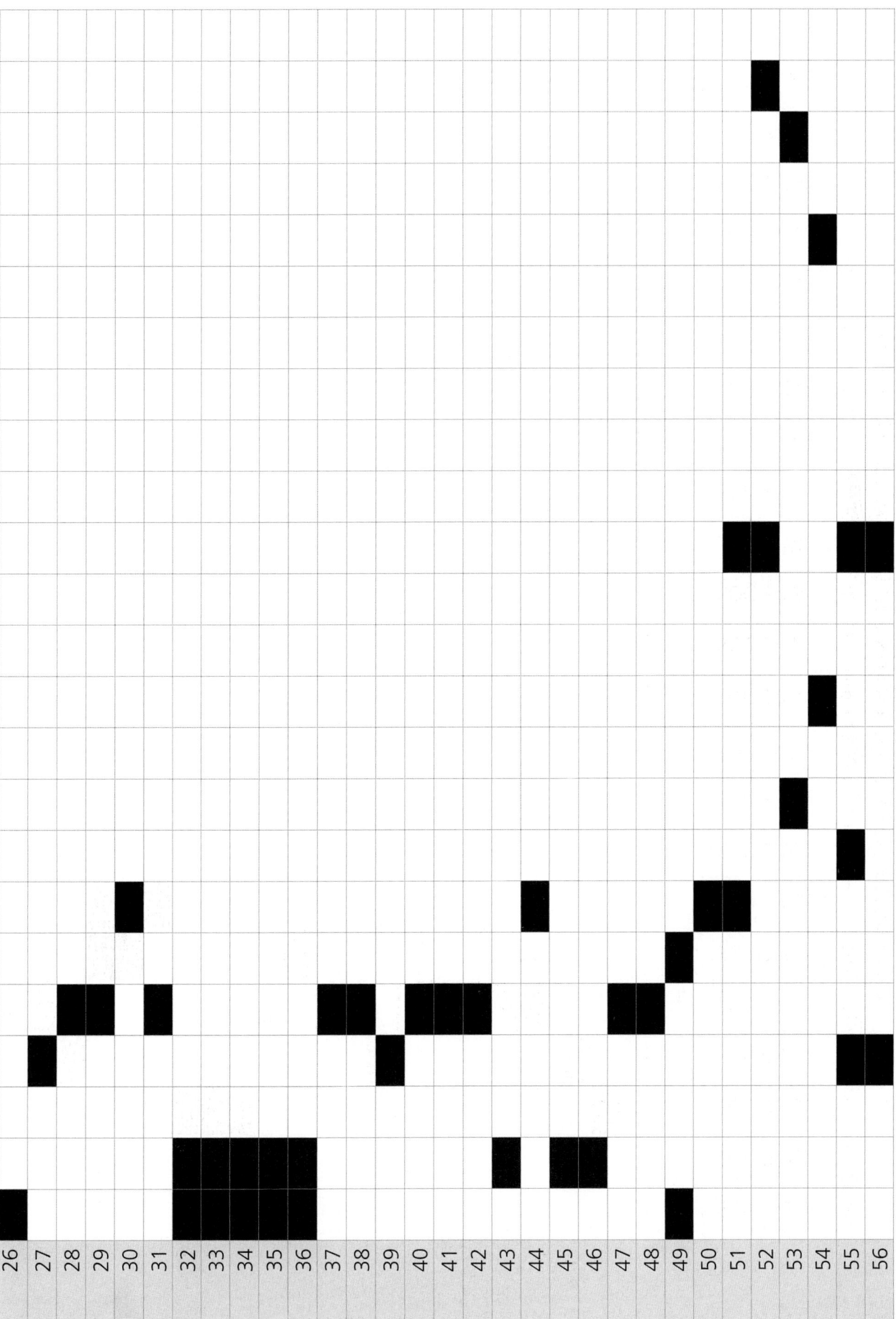